WOMEN'S INSTITUTE

BOOK
OF THE
HOME

JENNY KIELDSEN
WITH DAVID CARTER

SIMON & SCHUSTER
A CBS COMPANY

First published in Great Britain by
Simon & Schuster UK Ltd, 2006
A CBS Company

Copyright © this compilation WI
Enterprises Ltd, 2006. All rights
reserved.

ISBN 0 74326871 7

Simon & Schuster UK Ltd
Africa House
64-78 Kingsway
London
WC1B 6AH

Design by James Marks
Illustrations by Yvette Cocks
Index by Helen Peters
Printed and bound in China

CONTENTS

The book is dedicated to
all of my friends and family, who
have been such a huge support to
me during the time that I have
had cancer –it is because of you
that I have survived.
JK

THIS BOOK is going to change your life!

Well, perhaps make life a lot easier. It should answer most of those questions and queries that we all have about everyday life in and around the home. This is not a book telling you how to be a good housekeeper, but how to look very efficient and capable without a huge amount of effort!

The book is not stuffy or old fashioned, though some of the tips and hints have been around for years. We have endeavoured to make everything very 21st century. You'll be able to save time and money, and you can dip in and out of the book as you wish. We hope it will appeal to all ages, from those just off to college or leaving home to the newly living together, as well as to those who think they know it all, but might not.

Just some of the questions answered within the book are: how to identify wild food, get rid of moles, make lemon curd, clean leather upholstery, get rid of grease stains and hang wallpaper. There are recipes, useful addresses, washing tips, party game ideas and much more...

Can you resist not finding out?

THE HOME

This first chapter deals with general housework – washing, ironing, stain removal, cleaning (including windows, carpets, metals and fire surrounds) and looking after furniture. There are suggestions and useful tips for making light work of cleaning the kitchen, bathroom and bedrooms. 'Green' cleaning products are recommended where possible as they are healthier for the environment, and for you.

Try to get everyone in the family to pitch in with the household chores, or take turns with the more boring ones. Vacuum carpets at least once a week, and 'high traffic' areas more often.

LAUNDRY

KEEP THE LAUNDRY BASKET SMELLING FRESH

Sprinkle baking powder into the bottom of the dirty washing basket: to absorb any odours.

BEFORE YOU START WASHING

Check all pockets for money (if it's your partner's: finders keepers) and tissues that can ruin a whole wash. Button-up buttons and close zips. Check the care label for laundry instructions.

GET THE BEST FROM YOUR WASHING MACHINE

Do not overload it. There must be space for good circulation and movement of laundry in the drum or you won't get a good wash. Clear the filter at the bottom of the maxhine every six months or so to stop it getting clogged up.

REMOVE GREASY MARKS AND KEEP WHITES WHITE

Old-fashioned washing soda, a product we all seem to have forgotten, is still available in some supermarkets and from ironmongers. To perk up whites, put 2 tablespoons of washing soda in the washing powder channel of the machine with your chosen detergent and proceed as normal. As a professional cook, I can assure you that this works on chefs' jackets and aprons. Soak very greasy clothes overnight in a strong solution of 1 cup washing soda to 600 ml (1 pint) water. Drain, squeeze lightly and then wash the clothes as normal.

TO WASH VERY HEAVILY SOILED CLOTHES AND OVERALLS

Pour in a can of original Coca cola with the washing powder or liquid. The combination of sugar and syrup in the secret recipe works on the grease.

WASHING DELICATE LACE UNDERWEAR AND TIGHTS

Put them in an old pillowcase and machine wash as normal.

KEEP CORDUROY 'FLUFF FREE'

Turn garments inside out before putting into the washing machine. This also works well to prevent denim and black jeans fading.

REDUCE 'PILLING' (CLOTHES GETTING BOBBLY)

As above, try washing them inside out on a delicate wash, with a reduced spin cycle.

FADED COLOURS?

Sometimes fading is the result of a build up of washing powder within the fabric. Rinsing faded clothes in water with a good dash of vinegar added can get rid of the soap and bring the colour back. The same treatment can work on black clothes that have developed a whitish bloom.

HAND WASHING CLOTHES

Shampoo is excellent for hand washing. Use shampoos you bought and discovered don't suit your hair. Remember a little shampoo goes a long way and add it to the water before the clothes.

IF YOU RUN OUT OF FABRIC CONDITIONER

Use hair conditioner. Don't use fabric conditioner if you run out of hair conditioner though!

CRISP UP LACE/ NET CURTAINS

Add a tablespoon or so of salt to the final rinsing water. Dry these fabrics outside to keep them wrinkle free and fresh smelling.

TO HAND WASH SILK

Hand wash silk only if the label recommends it. I once ruined a dress by taking no notice of the label instructions. Add a tablespoon of vinegar to the final rinse to give the garment a professional crispness.

TO HAND WASH NECKTIES

The best advice is DON'T, but you can try removing food spots and spills. Slip a paper towel inside the tie to avoid wetting the reverse. Using hot water, a disposable cloth and a little washing-up liquid, dab the spot, letting the paper towel absorb any excess liquid. Use a hair dryer to dry the area as quickly as possible, to prevent a water mark forming and the tie from shrinking.

TO WASH A BASEBALL CAP

Put the cap in the top rack of the dishwasher and run a normal cycle. Leave it to air dry on a flat surface so that it retains its shape.

TO WASH A GLITTERY TOP

Spray with hair spray to make the glitter stay on. Then turn the garment inside out and hand wash in warm water. Drip dry.

TO MAKE WORN TOWELS FLUFFY

Soak them overnight in cold water with a cup of washing soda added. Do this in a bucket or use the soak cycle of the washing machine. Add detergent and wash as normal the next day. Wash towels in the hottest wash.

TO HAND WASH PURE WOOL JUMPERS OR SILK

Shampoo is excellent for delicate hand washing; adding a little hair conditioner to the final rinse works well too. Note that the final rinse should be in cold water.

TO MACHINE WASH KNITWEAR

Try placing machine-washable woollens inside a pillowcase to prevent them from stretching and going out of shape.

DRYING CLOTHES

Tumble dryers are a great asset in wet weather but they do use a lot of electricity. Try hanging your washing outdoors. There is pleasure in hanging out washing and watching it blowing in the wind, and the fresh smell of newly washed fabric is second to none. If you have a clothes pulley in a dry space, clothes will dry beautifully on this in winter, although it's not as quick as drying the clothes in a clothes dryer.

TO PREVENT MILDEW FORMING

The best way is to make sure that everything is bone dry before you put it away. Mildew produces microscopic spores that grow fast, especially on natural fabrics, such as cotton, linen and wool, and on leather, paper and wood.

STAIN REMOVAL

DEODORANT STAINS

Sponge white vinegar on the stain or rub with a cut lemon and leave for 30 minutes. Wash the item in the hottest wash that is safe for the fabric (check the care label).

UNDERARM STAINS ON COTTON CLOTHING

Dissolve 8–10 aspirins in a cup of warm water. Soak the underarm area of the garment in this for 30 minutes and then wash as normal. Be sure to throw the aspirin water away immediately.

DIRTY SHIRT COLLARS AND LIPSTICK STAINS

Rub a small amount of pale-coloured shampoo into the collar or lipstick mark before washing. Shampoo is designed to dissolve body oils.

HEAVY STAINS ON COTTON AND LINEN

Stains like blood, grease, ink, tea and coffee can be sprayed directly with liquid soda crystals (available in supermarkets or ironmongers) or soaked overnight in a strong solution of washing soda: allow 1 cup soda to 600 ml (1 pint) water. Then wash as normal.

SPILT NAIL VARNISH

Stretch the stained area of fabric over the top of a cup or glass and secure it with a rubber band. Drip on nail varnish remover and rub gently with a stainless steel teaspoon. This does take some time. Never use on silk.

For furnishing fabrics and carpets, immediately rub the area with a piece of cotton wool dampened with nail varnish remover. Be careful because this can take the colour out of your carpet or sofa. Best to paint your nails somewhere safe!

BLOOD STAINS ON CLOTHES

Soak for about 1 hour in salted lukewarm water. Allow longer if it is a bad stain and then wash as normal.

FOOD, RUST OR OTHER STAINS ON WHITE CLOTHES

Mix cream of tartar (available in the baking section of shops) with some lemon juice and dab on to the stain before washing in the normal way.

MILDEW STAINS

Mix salt and lemon juice, and rub well into the stained area before washing in the normal way.

TO REMOVE CANDLE WAX FROM CLOTHES

Chip off as much of the excess wax as you can. Protect the ironing board with a clean old cloth. Place the stained fabric on top and lay a sheet of brown paper over the mark. Brown paper bags are good, but make sure there is no printing on them. Iron the paper using a medium heat, without steam, and the wax will melt into the paper. Move the paper as it absorbs the wax, so that you are ironing a clean area.

RED WINE, COFFEE AND TEA
Soda water will remove all of these, especially if you act immediately. Lift any solid particles from the surface. Pour soda water on to the stain and blot with a dry cloth or disposable cloth and then wash as normal.

TO REMOVE CHEWING GUM
Start by putting the garment into a plastic bag and placing it in the freezer overnight. Remove from the freezer and immediately scrape off as much gum as you can with a blunt knife. Then rub in a little white vinegar and washing-up liquid and wash as normal.

MAKE-UP STAINS
Use a bar of beauty soap or shampoo (Dove brand is good). Wet the stain and rub in the soap well. Rinse with warm water. Wash in the normal way when the stain is removed.

IRONING

NO STEAM IRON?
Use hot water in a houseplant sprayer. For even dampness, spray each item all over and then roll up and leave for 20 minutes.

TO IRON EMBROIDERY
Damp the fabric as above and iron on the reverse side to make the embroidery stand out.

TO PRESS VELVET
Press on the reverse side: turn the fabric inside out and cover with a damp cotton cloth before ironing.

TO MAKE LINEN AND CLOTHES SMELL LOVELY
Add a few drops of your favourite toilet water to the water you pour into the iron.

TO PRESS A TIE
Lay the tie flat on the ironing board, cover it with a cotton cloth or tea towel and press lightly with the steam iron. Put the tie on a hanger to dry.

TO CLEAN AN IRON WITHOUT A NON-STICK SURFACE
Sprinkle table salt over a piece of brown paper or a brown paper bag. Heat the iron to hot on a dry, not a steam setting, and run it over the salt. Afterwards turn the iron to a high steam setting and run it over an old piece of clean fabric to remove any salt still left in the vent holes.

TO CLEAN A NON-STICK IRON
Make sure that the iron is not plugged in and is cold, and then apply a little toothpaste with a soft cloth. Rub it well into the surface with small circular motions, and then rinse with warm clean water.

ENERGY-EFFICIENT IRONING
To reduce ironing time and still get good results, try laying cooking foil (tin foil) under the ironing board cover. This will reflect heat up on to the clothes as you iron.

NO ACCESS TO AN IRON?

If you have wrinkled fabric and, for some reason, no iron, place the clothes on a hanger and hang in the bathroom. Fill the bath with hot water (or have a hot bath) and leave the water in. Close the door and leave for at least an hour – this encourages the creases to drop out of the garments.

FLOORS AND WALLS

WHICH VACUUM CLEANER?

Choose the vacuum cleaner that suits you and whoever else will use it. There are many different types, so look long and hard before you purchase. Compare upright, push-around cleaners with low-level, pull-behind models. Check the power rating and settings. Select tools and filters to suit your flooring and needs. Would a wet cleaner be useful?

VACUUM CLEANING

There has always been a debate in the 'home management' world as to whether to vacuum first or last. As far as I'm concerned it makes sense to do it last, once you're finished all the dusting and polishing.

TO REMOVE RED WINE, COFFEE AND TEA FROM CARPETS

As for clothing fabrics, soda water will remove all of these, especially if you act immediately. Lift any solids from the surface. Pour (or spray) on soda water and blot with a dry or disposable cloth. Do not be afraid to wet the carpet – it goes through countless dippings in water during manufacture.

TO REMOVE CANDLE WAX FROM CARPETS

Chip off as much excess wax as you can. Lay brown paper (paper bags are good, but make sure that there is no print on them) over the mark and gently press with a medium-hot iron on a dry, not steam, setting. Immediately you will see the wax being absorbed by the brown paper. Move the paper around as it gets greasy so that you don't re-deposit the wax on to the carpet.

TO REMOVE OIL, TAR AND BALL POINT PEN FROM CARPETS

WD40 is wonderfully useful for so many tasks. Carpets and floor coverings are made of so many different fibres that it is best to test a small area first to check that the fluid will not damage the carpet. Test a corner that will not be noticed. Vacuum the carpet thoroughly, spray WD40 over the marked area and leave for about 5 minutes. Dab with kitchen towel to remove the mark. Do not rub. Repeat as required. You may find that the smell hangs around for a couple of days but it will soon fade away.

TO REMOVE A DENT IN A CARPET

This simple technique really does work. Place an ice cube, or a tablespoon of cold water, in the dent: as the carpet pile slowly dries it will spring back to life.

TO ABSORB MUSTY CARPET ODOURS

Try mixing bicarbonate of soda with a few broken cloves, sprinkle on the carpet and leave overnight. Vacuum in the morning to leave the carpet smelling fresh.

TO REMOVE SMUDGES ON WALLPAPER

Put a good pinch of bicarbonate of soda on a wet cloth and rub the mark on the wallpaper gently. It should come off easily.

TO REMOVE GREASE SPOTS FROM WALLPAPER

Make a paste of cornflour and water. Apply the paste to the spot and allow it to dry, then gently brush off.

TO REMOVE MARKS FROM NON-WASHABLE WALLPAPER

Rub a scrunched up piece of white bread over the spots. You may have to repeat this a few times but it does work.

TO REMOVE CRAYON MARKS FROM WALLPAPER

Spray with WD40 and wipe the crayon marks away with paper towel. Take a soft cloth dipped in hot water and a little washing up liquid and rub with a circular motion to remove any marks.

FURNITURE AND SOFT FURNISHINGS

LOOKING AFTER WOODEN FURNITURE

Try not to use too much spray polish (containing silicone) on furniture, particularly on good wooden tables, sideboards, dressing tables, chests of drawers etc. It will build up on the surface and become streaky and smeary. Use traditional bees' wax polish occasionally – maybe 3–4 times a year. Leave it on for 30 minutes or so to give it a chance to sink into the wood. Give a good buff with a soft duster to remove the excess polish and achieve a good shine.

A proper occasional polish and a good dusting once a week is all the furniture needs. Try to use spray polish without chemicals harmful to the environment.

TO REMOVE OLD POLISH AND DIRT FROM FURNITURE

Use a cloth wrung out in warm water mixed with 1 tablespoon of malt vinegar to every 600 ml (1 pint) water. Allow this to dry and then re-polish. This mixture can also be used to remove the build up of spray polish on any type of surface.

TO REMOVE A WATER OR HEAT MARK FROM WOOD

Try massaging a small amount of mayonnaise into the stain. Leave overnight before wiping it off. You can also use butter or margarine, which is less smelly!

TO REMOVE STUBBORN MARKS FROM WOODEN FURNITURE

This tip is not for everyone, but if you do have a smoker around, you can make it count! For stubborn water or heat marks mix cigarette ash with the mayonnaise and use as above, but spend a little more time rubbing it in.

TO RESTORE DRIED-OUT WOOD

Dab some vaseline on a soft cloth and use to polish the furniture. The vaseline should feed and restore the dry wood.

TO CLEAN BAMBOO FURNITURE

Wipe with a cloth dipped into salty water. Then use a soft duster to rub in a little linseed oil (available in DIY stores).

TO CLEAN CANE FURNITURE AND WICKER CHAIRS

Make up a solution of $1/2$ cup washing soda to 600 ml (1 pint) warm water to wipe over the furniture. The soda hardens the cane and tightens sagging seats.

TO GET RID OF MUSTY SMELLS IN WOODEN CHESTS/WARDROBES

Put a slice of white bread in a bowl and pour in enough white vinegar to cover the bread. Stand the bowl inside the closed furniture for 24 hours or longer if the smell is still apparent.

TO STOP DUST SETTLING ON THE TELEVISION

Mix one part liquid fabric softener to four parts water. Use a soft cloth to apply this to the screen and buff dry with a duster. Make sure the power supply to the television is switched off before applying the moisture.

TELEVISION ECONOMY

Do make sure that the television and any similar electrical equipment is turned off at the switch on the receiver and not left on stand-by. This can consume huge amounts of electricity and, obviously, it becomes expensive.

TO FRESHEN UPHOLSTERY

Use a soft cloth soaked in a solution of washing soda, allowing 1 tablespoon soda to 600 ml (1 pint) hot water. Dab, don't scrub, the upholstery. Test a small area of fabric concealed from view for colourfastness before proceeding. Dry with a disposable cloth or a hairdryer.

TO CLEAN AND CARE FOR LEATHER UPHOLSTERY

Try to remove spots and spills as soon as they happen. Blot any excess liquid with a clean cloth or sponge, dry with a towel and allow to air dry.

Don't apply water to an oily or greasy mark; just wipe off any excess with a clean, dry cloth and leave. Don't use saddle soap or anything abrasive on leather.

At least once a week use a soft brush and then vacuum. Avoid positioning sofas and chairs near heat sources or in direct sunlight.

TO MAKE SURE A SOFA WEARS EVENLY

Rotate the cushions as often as you can, pulling them out, turning them over and repositioning them. Remember to give the sofa a good vacuum underneath the cushions and in all the nooks and crannies to remove crumbs and little bits of fluff.

TO HELP RELIEVE THE SMELL OF CIGARETTE SMOKE

If you or any guests still smoke, try burning scented candles to diminish the smell. Incense sticks help too, but avoid the sickly smelling ones. You can buy more natural incense sticks, such as those scented with lavender, jasmin and lemongrass.

METALS AND FIRE SURROUNDS

TO SHINE BRASS

A WI member recommends applying a little Worcestershire sauce using a soft cloth. Polish well and wash off any sauce residue with warm soapy water. Buff to a bright shine with a clean dry cloth.

TO CLEAN COPPER AND BRASS

Mix 3 tablespoons of salt with the juice of $1/2$ lemon and use to clean brass and copper. Rinse with warm water and buff to a shine with a soft cloth.

TO CLEAN SILVER

This old-fashioned tip for cleaning silver seems to work well, although I'm not sure why! Put a layer of aluminium foil in the washing up bowl or sink, lay the silver on top and pour over boiling water to cover. Add 3 tablespoons of bicarbonate of soda or washing soda and leave for 10 minutes. Drain, rinse and, finally, polish with a soft cloth.

TO CLEAN PEWTER

Dust it well and then wash in warm soapy water. Rinse and buff dry with a duster. DON'T use any polish on pewter.

TO CLEAN A SLATE HEARTH

Wash with warm soapy water and dry with a lint-free cloth. Buff the slate to a dull shine with a little sunflower oil on kitchen paper towel or on a soft cloth.

TO CLEAN METAL FIRE SURROUNDS

Penetrating fluid, such as WD40, is excellent for this. Spray on a small amount and wipe clean with kitchen towel.

WOODEN FIRE SURROUNDS

These should be looked after in the same way as wooden furniture, using bees' wax polish. The heat from the fire will dry out the wood, so feed and polish it more frequently than you would other furniture.

WINDOWS

If windows are really dirty, start by washing them down well with a bucket of warm water with a good squirt of washing-up liquid added. Dry with a chamois or an old linen tea towel. Make up a mixture of 2 tablespoons of white vinegar to 600 ml (1 pint) water in a spray bottle. Spray this over the windows and polish or buff them dry with paper towels, a lint-free rag or an old linen tea towel; or try the really old-fashioned method of polishing with newspaper. The print in the paper helps make the windows shiny. It is said that *The Daily Telegraph* is the best paper to use. If you read newspapers, and *The Telegraph* in particular, you will be well aware that the newsprint comes off all over your hands, so wear rubber gloves. My mother always said that because of the messy print you could never light a fire properly with *The Telegraph*!

TO CLEAN PAINTED AND UVPC (PLASTIC) WINDOW FRAMES

Wipe down regularly with a solution of $1/2$ cup washing soda to 600 ml (1 pint) water. Liquid soda is available as an alternative to soda crystals.

KITCHEN

WASHING-UP LIQUID

It is best to buy a good-quality concentrated brand. Cheap washing-up liquid is definitely not worth purchasing.

TO REMOVE BURNT FOOD FROM ROASTING TINS AND PANS

Fill the tin or pan with hot water and add 2–3 tablespoons of washing soda. Leave to soak overnight. Drain the tin or pan well and wash in the normal way. The burnt bits will come away easily. Wear rubber gloves when working with washing soda.

TO REMOVE BURNT BITS FROM SAUCEPANS

Fill the saucepan with warm water and add 2 tablespoons bicarbonate of soda. Bring to the boil and then continue to simmer until the burnt bits float to the surface.

TO REMOVE STAINS FROM NON-STICK COOKING PANS

Put 2 tablespoons bicarbonate of soda, $1/2$ cup white vinegar and 1 cup water in the pan. Bring to the boil, reduce the heat and simmer for 10–15 minutes. Drain and rinse the pan well in plenty of soapy water.

TO STOP MILK BURNING ON A SAUCEPAN

Try swirling cold water around a saucepan before heating the milk; this helps to prevent it from sticking to and burning the bottom of the saucepan .

TO CLEAN THE LIME SCALE (FUR) FROM INSIDE YOUR KETTLE

- Fill the kettle with water and put it in the freezer overnight. As the water defrosts the scale will come away with the ice.
- Pour in enough white or malt vinegar to cover the element (if it is electric with the element exposed) and bring it to the boil. Give the kettle a good shake to swirl the water, leave to cool and rinse thoroughly. Repeat as necessary.

STAINED FOOD PROCESSOR BLADE?

The food processor blade can become discoloured with frequent use and it is difficult to clean in a conventional way. Try soaking it by immersing the blade in a capful of bleach to 1 pint cold water, overnight or until clean. Then, rinse well and wash in boiling water and washing up liquid. Use an old toothbrush to scrub all the difficult corners.

TO CLEAN AND FRESHEN A WASTE DISPOSAL UNIT

Sprinkle a few ice cubes into the unit. Switch it on and keep the tap running. This sharpens up the blades. Then finish by putting some lemon or orange peel down to make it smell fresh

TO KEEP DRAINS RUNNING FREELY

Pour 1/2 cup bicarbonate of soda down the sink and then follow with 1 cup white vinegar. Leave this, without rinsing, for 15 minutes. Then pour down a kettle full of boiling water.

REMOVING RUBBER GLOVES

If your hands have become hot and sweaty in rubber gloves, try rinsing them under cold running water. This will cool your hands and make the gloves come off more easily.

TO STOP WATER GETTING INTO YOUR RUBBER GLOVES

Turn back a cuff on the gloves, at the wrists. When you lift or tip up your arms the water will run into the cuff and not all over you.

TO CLEAN THE MICROWAVE

Put some slices of lemon into a glass bowl. Half-fill with water and cook on high for 3 minutes. The steam will loosen the dirt and the lemon will make the microwave smell fresh.

TO REMOVE RUST FROM A KNIFE

Peel a large onion and stick the rusty part of the knife into it. Move the blade backwards and forwards several times to help the onion juice do its work.

TO REMOVE TEA OR COFFEE STAINS FROM CUPS AND MUGS

- Fill the mugs with water and add a tiny splash of bleach. Leave for 20 minutes and wash and rinse thoroughly.
- Using kitchen towel, rub the stained areas with a little salt or bicarbonate of soda. The abrasive action will remove the stains.
- Soak for an hour or overnight in a solution of washing soda, using 1 cup soda to 600 ml (1 pint) water. Wash and rinse thoroughly, as you would normally.

TO CLOSE OPEN FOOD PACKETS

Rather than buying expensive purpose-made closers, use wooden clothes pegs. These are particularly good on slippery plastic packs and work just as well on food bags for the freezer. Plastic pegs are also useful for pinching some bags closed.

TO REMOVE RUST FROM WORK SURFACES

This is useful for Formica and plastic laminates. Make a paste of cream of tartar (from the baking section of shops) and fresh lemon juice. Apply the paste to the rust spot and leave for about 30 minutes. Scrub the surface with a nylon scouring pad and rinse. Repeat if necessary.

TO KEEP THE BOTTOM OF THE OVEN OR GRILL PAN CLEAN

Lay a sheet of foil in the bottom of your oven or grill pan. Be sure to change it regularly.

SMOKING OVEN?

If something boils over in the oven – particularly fat and oil – it will start smoking immediately. As soon as you can, sprinkle a thick layer of salt over the spillage. The smoke and smell will stop at once. Next day you'll be able to lift out the whole 'mess' with a fish slice.

COPING WITH A CHIP PAN FIRE

Switch off the heat. Do not move the pan. NEVER throw water over it. Cover the pan completely to exclude air. Fire needs oxygen to burn, so without air the flames will die out. Use an item that will not immediately burn: a large lid, a baking tray, large wooden chopping board, door mat or thick, folded damp cloth. Leave the cover in place – do not lift it until the oil has cooled.

TURNING OFF THE FRIDGE OR FREEZER

If you are turning off a fridge or freezer for any length of time, prop open the door. This lets air in and prevents the inside from becoming smelly or mouldy.

A SWEET-SMELLING FRIDGE

Strong-smelling foods will taint mild ingredients. Cut melon in particular will taint everything in the fridge, especially milk and butter. Be sure to cover melon and other cut fruit and vegetables with cling film. Put a dessertspoonful of bicarbonate of soda in a small dish (a ramekin is ideal) and place in the fridge. This works wonders by absorbing food odours. Change the soda about every 2 weeks. My cousin swears by a used tea bag, air-dried and placed on a shelf. For really strong odours, put fresh coffee grounds into an open container and leave overnight.

TO SEPARATE STACKED GLASSES

Stand the bottom glass in hot water (not boiling) and pour cold water into the top glass. Twist the glasses very lightly and you should be able to pull them apart easily.

TO CLEAR THE AIR OF BURNT-FOOD SMELLS

Boil a few lemon slices (or lemon zest) in a saucepan of water for a few minutes.

TO STOP THE SMELL OF FRIED FOOD HANGING AROUND

This works, even when frying fish. Place a small bowl of white vinegar next to the cooker or fryer while you are cooking.

TO STOP STEEL WOOL PADS GOING RUSTY

Pop the lightly used pads in a small polythene bag and store in the freezer.

TO CLEAN MARBLE WORK SURFACES

Dust or wipe the surfaces with a damp cloth. For caked-on spots, sprinkle on some baking powder and rub with a damp sponge.

You can also use a mixure of one part liquid fabric softener to two parts water to clean the surfaces thoroughly and then finish by polishing them with a soft cloth to dry.

BATHROOM

TO CLEAN A DIRTY BATH

If the bath is really dirty and greasy, fill it with water, add several cups of washing soda and leave for 2 –3 hours or overnight. Wearing rubber gloves, use a stiff brush and you will find this will clean the dirtiest of baths.

Plastic baths should not be cleaned with abrasive cleaners as it will mark them.

TO CLEAN TAPS

A small amount of shaving cream on a soft cloth is good for cleaning taps or other chrome fittings.

BROWNISH STAINS FROM DRIPPING TAPS?

A good rub with a mixture of salt and vinegar will remove the stains easily. This mixture also works on chrome taps; finish them by polishing with a dry cloth or, best of all, a chamois leather.

TO CLEAN THE LAVATORY

Start with the seat and cover. There is debate about whether or not to use a brush inside the pan: I do, with bleach, but make sure the brush is cleaned afterwards. Otherwise, wear rubber gloves, use a special toilet cleaner, a cloth and elbow grease. Keep the cloth and gloves somewhere in the bathroom, solely for this purpose.

A quick fix for cleaning the water line and below is to pop in two denture cleaning tablets and leave overnight. A can's-worth of cola left overnight also works well!

TO REMOVE BUILD UP FROM SHOWER HEADS AND TAPS

Half fill a small plastic bag with scrunched up kitchen paper, pour in enough white vinegar to soak the paper completely. Place the bag over the shower head or tap so that the end nozzle is covered with the vinegar paper and tie in place or secure with an elastic band. Leave the bag overnight and then the lime scale can be wiped away easily. If necessary, poke out any difficult bits with a wooden cocktail stick.

TO CLEAN SPACES AROUND SHOWER DOOR TRACKS

Wrap a cloth around a small, slim screwdriver, dip it into bleach and you should be able to fit it into most places. Cotton buds are good for those awkward small corners.

TO CLEAN AND POLISH MARBLE SURFACES

Mix one part fabric softener with two parts water and use to thoroughly clean the surfaces, then polish off with a soft cloth.

TO REMOVE SCUM OR MILDEW FROM A SHOWER CURTAIN

Pour 1 cup white vinegar into the fabric softener drawer. Use your normal detergent, run the cycle (40°c) and re-hang the curtain immediately. It is a good idea to put some light-coloured towels in with the curtain.

TO REMOVE MOULD FROM TILES AROUND BATH AND SHOWER

Use a cotton bud dipped in bleach to clean small corners or use a cottonwool ball for larger areas and leave the bleach on for a few minutes. Be sure to wear rubber gloves and not too splash your clothes when using bleach – I speak from experience.

TO CLEAN RUBBER 'NON SLIP' BATH OR SHOWER MATS

Put it in the washing machine with 2–3 bath towels and run a 40°c wash cycle.

MIRROR MAGIC

To stop the mirror steaming up when you shower or have a bath, rub a few drops of shampoo, shaving cream or washing-up liquid on the glass.

TO KEEP THE SOAP DISH CLEAN

When you have thoroughly cleaned the soap dish, dip a cottonwool pad or kitchen paper in a little baby oil and wipe this all over the dish. The oil will repel the water making it easier to keep the dish clean.

TO FRESHEN FLANNELS AND SPONGES

Soak them in a solution of washing soda, about $\frac{1}{2}$ cup to 600 ml (1 pint) water. This will get rid of any greasy deposits.

TO KEEP DRAINS RUNNING FREELY

Pour $\frac{1}{2}$ cup bicarbonate of soda down the sink, followed by a cup of white vinegar. Leave this, without rinsing, for 15 minutes and then pour down a kettle full of boiling water.

OLD TOOTHBRUSHES

Don't throw away old toothbrushes – wash them in bleach to make sure they are clean, then rinse and dry them. They are incredibly useful for lots of household cleaning jobs, particularly for getting into otherwise inaccessible crevices in kitchen equipment, such as food processors and blenders.

EMBARRASSING TOILET SMELLS?

A lighted match will eliminate most odours. Do not leave matches in the bathroom or cloakroom if there are children in the house (or visiting).

BEDROOM

MATTRESS CARE

Turn the mattress over at least twice a year to spread out the wear. Don't do this on your own though, as a mattress is cumbersome, flexible and it seems to have a mind of its own when it's being turned.

TO FRESHEN A MATTRESS

● Use the upholstery attachment on your vacuum cleaner to remove all dust and fluff. Remove any marks with a drop of washing-up liquid in warm water. Do be sure to dry the mattress thoroughly using paper towels or a hair dryer.
● Sprinkle generously with bicarbonate of soda and leave to stand for a few hours. Vacuum off the soda.

TO KEEP CLOTHES WRINKLE FREE

Do not fill your wardrobe to bursting. If you don't have much space for hanging, pack out-of-season clothes in suitcases or drawers. Remember to protect against moths (see page 25)

TO MAKE WARDROBE SPACE

If you have not worn something for at least two years, try it on and make the decision to wear it tomorrow or throw it away. It is best to give good clothes to a charity shop. If you have something that is still new or virtually new and was the wrong choice, placing it in a nearly new shop is an option. These shops pay different rates and terms.

BED LINEN SIZES
Single fitted sheet 200 cm x 137 cm
Single flat sheet 254 cm x 178 cm
Single duvet cover 200 cm x 137 cm
Double fitted sheet 200 cm x 200 cm
Double flat sheet 254 cm x 228 cm
Double duvet cover 200 cm x 200 cm
King size fitted sheet 225 cm x 220 cm
King size flat sheet 259 cm x 269 cm
King size duvet cover 225 cm x 220 cm
Super king size fitted sheet 260 cm x 220 cm
Super king size flat sheet 295 x 270
Super king size duvet 260cm x 220cm

Usually, they'll display your item for about one month and if it sells you receive about half the price. This is better than nothing and you'll feel less guilty about making the mistake in the first place.

TO KEEP YOUR WARDROBE SMELLING FRESH

Put only clean clothes in the wardrobe as something dirty will soon contaminate everything else. Never return laundered clothes to the wardrobe unless they are absolutely bone dry. Hook lavender bags or cedar wood rings over coat hangers for good smells and to help deter moths.

SCENTED CLOTHES AND UNDIES

Remove those scent 'test strips' from magazines and put in your underwear drawer, or spike on to a clothes hanger for your wardrobe.

EVERYDAY HINTS

This chapter consists of all kinds of straightforward hints and tips to make life easier and save time and money – how can you resist that? Browse through the entries, which will spark off heaps of great ideas. Then, when a particular problem or situation arises, you will remember these snippets and think: 'Aha, I'm sure I read how to sort that out in the *Book of the Home*.

For heat rash or stings, use calamine lotion or anti-histamine cream to cool the skin. The good old dock leaf is worth a try on a nettle sting. These big, broad green leaves usually grow near nettles.

GOOD IDEAS

TO MOVE HEAVY FURNITURE

If you have to move very heavy furniture but do not have enough manpower to help, find some really thick polythene (sacks are suitable) and place them under each leg or corner. You will then be able to slide the furniture into position quite easily.

TO KEEP YOUR TELEPHONE CLEAN AND HEALTHY

Dip a cotton wool ball in a good-quality mouthwash or TCP (undiluted) and apply thoroughly to the phone receiver. Use a cotton bud for small corners. Do not rinse off. This is great advice if anyone in the family has a cold or cough.

TO REMOVE A BROKEN LIGHT BULB FROM THE SOCKET

Unplug the light if it is a lamp or make sure that it is turned off at the switch. Take a large bar of damp soap and push this up into the jagged edges of the bulb. Twist counter clockwise and you should be able to remove the remains of the bulb as you pull out the bar of soap.

TO CLEAN UP BROKEN GLASS

A thick slice of bread will pick up all the little broken shards of glass that scatter everywhere. Be careful, though, and do not turn the slice of bread over.

TO TEST A SMOKE ALARM

(If you don't regularly burn toast!) Gently move a lighted candle beneath the alarm; if it doesn't go off, replace the batteries.

TO RE-VITALISE A SQUASHED PING-PONG BALL

Provided that the ball doesn't have a hole in it, heat it in boiling water for a few minutes. The air inside will expand and push out the dent.

TO PREVENT NEWSPAPER CUTTINGS FROM YELLOWING

Mix 1 tablespoons Milk of Magnesia with 600 ml (1 pint) soda water and put this in the fridge overnight. Pour into a shallow tray and submerge the cuttings in the liquid for 1 hour. Remove the newspaper and leave to dry overnight, then date and store them out of sunlight.

EMERGENCY HELP FOR WALKING IN ICY WEATHER

If it snows or is very icy and you don't have Wellington boots or the right shoes, try putting an old pair of thick socks on over a pair of shoes. This helps to give a good grip and prevent you from slipping and sliding as you walk.

TO TIE PARCELS TIGHTLY

When wrapping parcels ready for posting, dip the string in warm water and then tie the knots. As the string dries it will shrink, leaving a tight knot.

TO RE-USE ENVELOPES

Make use of all those unwanted addressed envelopes that you receive in the post for paying bills.

Place a sticky label over the address and re-use the envelope (remember to put on a stamp).

TO SHARPEN SCISSORS

Try cutting a sheet of fine sandpaper or emery paper into small pieces. The gritty surface will sharpen the blades. Alternatively, cut through a double layer of foil.

TO CLEAN BABY RATTLES AND TEETHING RINGS

Tie them together and wash in the top tray of the dishwasher.

TO CLEAN STUFFED-FABRIC TOYS THAT CANNOT BE WASHED

Place in a plastic bag and dust heavily with bicarbonate of soda or salt. Work the dry ingredients well over the toys and shake vigorously for a few minutes. Leave overnight or shake a few times a day for several days to remove dust, dirt and smells. Then use a clean brush and brush the toys thoroughly outdoors.

TO CLEAN OR DUST OBJECTS WITH SMALL PARTS

Use a paintbrush to dust the nooks and crannies of toys or artifacts with small fiddly parts. Do this outside if the object is very dusty. Alternatively, put a pair of tights or a stocking over the attachment end of a vacuum cleaner so that when you clean, it doesn't suck up small pieces.

TO KEEP MOTHS OUT OF CLOTHES

Lots of ideas here. You can use bought mothballs, but these are very expensive and the smell, which will remind you of very old ladies, is difficult to get rid of.
● Try placing good, scented soap (unwrapped) among the clothes, for example in pockets.
● Lavender oil on cotton wool balls, again placed among the clothes, is very good.
● Cedar wood chips, available with barbecue equipment, can be used. Pop these into a fine fabric sachet so that the cedar oils do not touch your clothes and pack them with your winter woollies.
● Conkers! An old wives tale that is worth trying: take the conkers out of their prickly shells and pop them in with your winter woollies.
● You can also try killing moths by putting the clothes in the freezer for 24 hours. Remember to wrap the clothes well in polythene bags first.

TO REVITALISE STICKY ZIPS

If a zip will not pull up easily, try rubbing it with a bar of soap or a candle. Zip it up and down a couple of times to lubricate the teeth. A little penetraing fluid, such as WD40, is also good on metal zips.

TO REMOVE STICKY RESIDUE LEFT BY STICKERS OR LABELS

This is a particularly good if your children put sticky labels all over their bedrooms and bedroom furniture, or for labels on jam jars. Peel of the top layer of paper and spray the layer stuck to the surface with penetrating fluid, such as WD40. Wipe off with kitchen paper or scrape the surface gently with a knife.

TO TIGHTEN A LOOSE TIN LID

Sometimes a lid on a favourite storage tin suddenly becomes loose. If you want the contents to continue to keep airtight and dry, apply a strip of sticky tape all the way around the inside rim.

TO CLEAN MIRRORS

Never spray water on a mirror as moisture can get into the edges and then behind the mirror. This will spoil the silvering and result in dark spots on the mirror.

Use a mixture of half vinegar and half water. Wet a sponge, soft cloth or paper towel with the solution and use it to clean the mirror; then buff dry.

POSITIONING MIRRORS IN YOUR HOME

Mirrors are not only for looking at yourself – they are great for bringing light into your home. Place them opposite or near a window to reflect light into a room or space. A large mirror, or a whole mirrored wall, can widen a narrow hall, or make a small room seem a lot bigger.

TO CLEAN GLASS DECANTERS, VASES AND SCENT BOTTLES

Fill with warm water and pop in 1–2 denture cleaning tablets. Leave overnight and you will be able to rinse the dirt and stains away. Repeat the process to remove more stubborn marks.

COOLING SUN-TAN LOTION

When sun bathing at home, what a pleasure it is to keep the cream in the fridge and apply it when it is really cold.

SUPERMARKET PARKING

This is very personal to me but it might also be of interest to you. I always park where there are plenty of spaces as far away as possible from the entrance. I select my trolley and by the time I enter the store I have passed everyone getting flustered over trying to prize their cars into tiny spaces and themselves out of barely open doors. I then take great heart that I am arriving calmer and getting a little exercise by pushing the trolley back to my car.

LOOKING AFTER GLASSES

When washing glasses by hand, rather than putting them straight on to the draining board, lay a clean linen tea towel on the surface first. This stops the glasses from slipping and helps to drain the water from them. To make glass really sparkly and clean, add a splash of vinegar or washing soda to the final rinsing water.

CHIPPED DRINKING GLASSES?

There are companies that will re-grind chipped glasses. This is worthwhile for good-quality, expensive glassware, particularly cut glass. It is also excellent if the glasses are part of a set that you don't want to replace. The professional grinding is hardly noticeable. Ask in the china and glassware department of a large store to find out whether they offer this service.

TO LOOK AFTER WOODEN SALAD BOWLS

Do not immerse them in water for more than a few seconds, and then dry them thoroughly. Dip kitchen paper in olive oil or vegetable oil and give the bowl a good rub all over. This will prevent the wood from drying and cracking.

SQUEAKY FLOORBOARDS?

Try sprinkling talcum powder between the floorboards.

CLING FILM

If possible, buy catering size rolls of cling film in cutter boxes – they are available in some supermarkets, from discount stores or 'cash and carry' outlets. They come in many widths and are much easier to handle than small packets. You will soon notice how unwieldy and over priced those small boxes are.

TO SAVE MONEY ON YOUR WATER BILL

If your family is not large, or you live alone, having a water meter fitted is often very worthwhile. This way you pay only for what you use and not for what the water supplier estimates you use! Some meters are free; for others you pay a small fee.

Check for, and mend, dripping taps – you would be amazed how much water can be dripped away and wasted (see page 84).

TIPS FOR CANDLES

● To increase the life of candles, try popping them in the freezer for 2–3 hours before use.
● To make it easier to fit a candle into a stick or candle holder, dip the end into hot water until it is soft enough to fit on to a spike or into a holder.

TO REVIVE A BALLPOINT PEN

Try dipping the writing end in boiling water for a moment or two to revitalize it.

FELT-TIP PEN TRICKS

Remember to store felt-tip pens with caps on and facing down. If a felt-tip pen stops working, try dipping the nib in a little vinegar.

TO REPAIR A LOOSE BROOM HANDLE

Try wrapping sticky tape around the end of the broom handle, then push it back into the hole in the brush head with a twisting action.

WHAT TO DO WITH A WARPED WOODEN BREAD BOARD

Try placing it on a flat surface, warped side down, and covering it with a wet tea towel. Leave for at least 24 hours.

TO RENOVATE CHIPPED PICTURE FRAMES

If you have little chips or small bits knocked off the edges of picture frames (including wood and painted wood), try using a felt-tip pen in a matching colour to cover the mark. You might need to renew this occasionally. This is particularly good on wood as the ink sinks into the surface.

FOR A SWEET-SMELLING HOUSE

Boil some water in a saucepan, turn off the heat and add a broken cinnamon stick and a few cloves. The steam will carry the aroma around the house.

To banish the smell of smoke, throw some orange or lemon peel on the open fire, if you have one.

SHOES AND HANDBAGS

TO COVER MARKS ON HEELS

Heavy, wide marker pens are particularly good for this. Available in most colours to match shoes, you will need to re-apply the colour occasionally.

TO MAKE SOLES ON NEW SHOES LESS SLIPPERY

Score the soles lightly with the prongs of a fork or use the point of a sharp knife.

TO REMOVE SALT MARKS FROM LEATHER FOOTWEAR

Wipe the leather with a mixture of half water and half white distilled vinegar. Leave the shoes or boots to dry and then polish in the normal way.

TO DRY WET SHOES

Stuff the shoes with newspaper. The paper will absorb the damp and help to keep the shoes in shape. For pale-coloured shoes, wrap a tea towel around the newspaper so that the print doesn't stain the shoes.

NO POLISH TO MATCH YOUR SHOES?

When you don't have polish of the right colour for your shoes, you can spray a little furniture polish on to a rag, rub it well into the shoes and buff them to a shine. In a real hurry you can use face or baby wipes to polish shoes and then buff them well.

TO CLEAN PATENT LEATHER SHOES AND HANDBAGS

The main problem with patent leather is that it gets dry and cracks. Rubbing in Vaseline is the way to prevent this. If the leather is really dry, leave the Vaseline on for a while before rubbing off using a soft dry cloth.

TO REPLACE THE PLASTIC TIPS ON SHOELACES

Try dipping the ends into clear or coloured nail varnish. This will stop them fraying and you will be able to thread them through the eyeholes easily.

TO STOP SHOES SQUEAKING

If they have leather soles, try rubbing a little linseed oil on the soles, particularly where they join the shoes. Do be careful when walking on pale carpets for a few days though.

TO PREVENT SMELLY SHOES

A good sprinkle of bicarbonate of soda inside the shoe neutralises most odours. It is especially good in smelly trainers.

TO CLEAN LEATHER HANDBAGS

Rinse a cloth in warm water, wring out and lather with a bar of moisturising soap (Dove is good). Rub well into the leather, rinsing the cloth as needed, and buff dry with a soft duster. You can then polish the bag with shoe polish or cream, but make sure the polish is thoroughly absorbed and the handbag buffed, so that it doesn't mark your clothes.

TO CLEAN A SUEDE HANDBAG AND SHOES

Use a special suede brush (available in shoe shops and shoe menders) to keep the nap smooth. To remove grease stains, try rubbing gently with a little neat white vinegar on a soft cloth. Allow it to dry in sunlight and brush to restore.

TO CLEAN THE INSIDE OF YOUR HANDBAG

Something we all need to do more often! Empty out all the contents (all sorts of mislaid items may come to light), give the bag a good shake and then use a small vacuum attachment to remove the dust and dirt.

TO PREVENT LEATHER HANDBAGS GETTING MOULDY

Vigorously rub in a thin layer of Vaseline and then buff up with a soft clean cloth.

HOLIDAYS

TO ORGANISE YOUR SUITCASE

If you are a frequent traveller or moving locations every two three days, pack to suit your travels. For instance, put all your underwear in the same corner every time you travel; do the same with tops, bottoms and clothes for specific occasions. Pack clothes in the order you will be wearing them – if your first stopover is a warm place and the climate cooler as you progress, put warmer clothes at the bottom, and light items on top. This may seem a bit of a palaver at first, but after a few trips, if you always put things in the same place, you will be able to put your hand on the right garment almost blindfolded!

PERFECT PACKING

Put everything you want to take with you out on your bed. Fold items into neat piles before putting them into the case, taking note of the advice about organising your suitcase.

TO ENSURE YOUR HOME SMELLS FRESH ON YOUR RETURN

Buy wintergreen oil from the health food shop, put a few drops on to cotton wool balls and place these into various places around the house. Never place oil-soaked items directly on wooden surfaces but in non-absorbent containers.

TO IDENTIFY YOUR SUITCASE EASILY ON ARRIVAL

This is useful on the carousel at the airport. Have you noticed how almost everyone owns a dark suitcase, making it virtually impossible to pick out yours?
● Buy a bright-coloured case and you'll see it approaching from a distance on the carousel. The rigid plastic type is available in loud colours and a good-quality one will stand up to years of hard wear.

● Buy bright case straps or tie bright webbing or ribbons around a dark case.

IF YOU PLAN TO SHOP ON HOLIDAY
It is a good idea to pack a suitable flat bag at the bottom of your suitcase ready to hold your holiday shopping. If you're flying you might end up having to pay an excess baggage charge.

TRAVEL IRONS
Travel irons are very useful, but if you don't have one, try hanging creased clothes in the bathroom and fill the bath with hot water (or take a bath or have a shower). Close the door to keep the steam in the room. Leave the water in the bath for at least an hour. Leave the clothes hanging overnight; this helps to remove most of the creases.

TO KEEP SWIMWEAR LASTING LONGER
After swimming in a chlorinated pool always rinse your costume in cold water. Adding a little fabric conditioner helps too. This also works for sea water on costumes.

TO REMOVE SAND FROM BODIES
Try sprinkling baby powder on your body when you are ready to come off the beach and the sand should fall of easily.

TO EASE SUNBURN
Mix a solution of half cider vinegar and half tepid water. Spray this on for instant relief. A cool bath helps, with a shake of bicarbonate of soda or salt in the water to soothe the stinging. Vitamin E cream is great on sunburnt skin.
● If you're lucky enough to be in a country where the plant Aloe Vera grows, squeeze some sap from the leaf for instant relief.

NO PLUG IN THE BATH OR SINK?
Pack an old squash ball as it can be squashed to fit into most sizes of plughole.

HOLIDAY WASHING SUPPLIES
Decant clothes washing liquid and some fabric conditioner into small plastic shampoo bottles with screw tops for ease of packing. A coat hanger with pegs at each end is useful for drip-drying (you will find that hotel hangers often have small straight tops that fit into catches in the wardrobes).

PAPAYA FOR AN UPSET TUMMY
If you are in a hot country where ripe papayas (sometimes known as pawpaws) are available, you will find that these delicious fruits are great healers. The black shiny seeds are very helpful too; chew them – they are crunchy and taste slightly peppery.

A GREAT MIDGE REPELLENT
This tip is particularly good for the west coast of Scotland. A long established Avon product called 'Soft & Fresh Dry Oil Body Spray' has a huge reputation for discouraging midges. It is not sold as insect repellent and is not available in shops. Order from your 'Avon Lady' online at www.avon.uk.com or 0845 6014040.

CLOTHING AND SHOE SIZES

WOMEN'S SUITS, DRESSES AND COATS

British	8	10	12	14	16	18	20
European	36	38	40	42	44	46	48
USA		6	8	10	12	14	16	18

MEN'S SUITS AND COATS

British	36	38	40	42	44	46
European	46	48	51	54	56	59
USA	36	38	40	42	44	46

SHOE SIZES

Women's shoes

British	4	$4\frac{1}{2}$	5	$5\frac{1}{2}$	6	$6\frac{1}{2}$	7
European	37	$37\frac{1}{2}$	38	39	$39\frac{1}{2}$	40	$40\frac{1}{2}$
USA	$5\frac{1}{2}$	6	$6\frac{1}{2}$	7	$7\frac{1}{2}$	8	$8\frac{1}{2}$

Men's shoes

British	7	$7\frac{1}{2}$	8	9	10	11
European	$40\frac{1}{2}$	41	42	43	$44\frac{1}{2}$	46
USA	$7\frac{1}{2}$	8	$8\frac{1}{2}$	$9\frac{1}{2}$	$10\frac{1}{2}$	$11\frac{1}{2}$

METRIC TO IMPERIAL CONVERSION EQUATIONS

TEMPERATURE

To convert centigrade to Fahrenheit, multiply by 1.8 and add 32

$$°C \times 1.8 + 32 = °F$$

To convert Fahrenheit to centigrade, subtract 32 and multiply by 0.55

$$F - 32 \times 0.55 = C$$

LENGTH, DISTANCE AND AREA

	multiply by
inches to centimetres	2.54
centimetres to inches	0.39
feet to metres	0.30
metres to feet	3.28
yards to metres	0.91
metres to yards	1.09
miles to kilometres	1.61
kilometres to miles	0.62
acres to hectares	0.40
hectares to acres	2.47

WEIGHT

	multiply by
ounces to grams	28.35
grams to ounces	0.035
pounds to kilograms	0.45
kilograms to pounds	2.21
British tons to kilograms	1016
US tonnes to kilograms	907

- A British ton = 2240 lb
- A US tonne = 2000 lb

VOLUME

	multiply by
British gallons to litres	4.55
litres to British gallons	0.22
US gallons to litres	3.79
litres to US gallons	0.26

- 5 British gallons = 6 US gallons
- A litre is slightly more than a US quart and slightly less than a British quart.

FOOD &
ENTERTAINING

This section is packed with general cooking tips, as well as helpful hints on using the microwave, making the most of wild food, using herbs, making jam and marmalade, ideas for sandwiches and a checklist of oven cooking temperatures. There are also useful tips for specific occasions, as well as some quick and simple snacks to serve with drinks, at children's parties, Christmas and Easter.

Social gatherings can be enjoyable for everyone. With a little pre-planning and simple food you will be able to spend more time with your guests than in the kitchen.

INGREDIENTS

WEIGHING INGREDIENTS

If you still work in imperial measures (pounds and ounces), it is good to note that one lightly heaped tablespoon of flour or sugar is equal to an ounce.

WEIGHING TREACLE OR SYRUP

Three tips here:
1. If it is to be melted, weigh the syrup in the saucepan – put the pan on the scales, put the scales back to zero and add the syrup.
2. To slide the syrup or treacle off a measuring spoon easily, dip the tablespoon into flour and then into the treacle.
3. Finally, heat a tablespoon in a gas flame or in boiling water and then immediately use it to scoop out the syrup.

TO MAKE PASTRY WITH WHOLEMEAL FLOUR

Using wholemeal flour on its own makes pastry very heavy and dull. Use a quarter cornflour or plain flour to three-quarters wholemeal flour to lighten the mix and make lovely short pastry.

TO CHECK IF AN EGG IS FRESH

Fill a bowl with cold water and put in the egg. A really fresh egg will sink to the bottom. One that floats is definitely off – throw it away. Anything in the middle is acceptable.

TO STOP BOILED EGGS CRACKING

Add 1 tablespoon vinegar or 1 teaspoon of salt to the water in which the eggs are to be boiled.

TO SHELL HARD-BOILED EGGS

To prevent the eggs from going black around the yolk and to peel them easily, as soon as they are cooked, drain and run under cold water. Tap them gently to crack the shells for easy peeling. Leave under cold water or in several changes of cold water for 5–6 minutes, then remove the shells.

TO USE UP SOUR MILK

If milk turns sour (and this is when it smells or tastes sour not when it has reached the best-before date) it is excellent for making scones.

PARMESAN CHEESE

Please don't buy ready grated Parmesan cheese in little tubs. It is awful and can smell like sick and/or look and feel like sawdust. Buy a whole piece of good Parmesan and keep it well wrapped (cling film and foil) in either the fridge or freezer. When required, just unwrap and grate as much as you need. A micro-plane grater is excellent for this.

BUYING OLIVE OIL

Always try to buy the best olive oil you can afford. Usually the darker green the oil, the richer the flavour. Avoid oil in green bottles that disguise the real colour of the oil. The best-quality supermarket own brand is nearly always better than the well-known brands.

Reserve your best – or flavoured– oil for dressings or to use on its own and use a cheaper one for cooking. Olive oil is great on toast instead of butter, and healthy too.

BUYING PASTA

A good brand of dried pasta is far superior to the fresh pasta offered in supermarkets; the latter tends to be wet and claggy when cooked. The Italians mostly use dried and make their own only for special occasions. They buy fresh when they can from a good local producer. Dried pasta also keeps better and is a good store cupboard basic.

CHOOSING PASTA SHAPES

- Short tubular pasta (e.g. rigatoni, penne, macaroni) is best used in baked dishes with vegetables, cheese. and meat.
- Smooth long pasta (e.g. spaghetti, linguine) is best with sauces like Bolognese, tomato and clams as these keep the pasta slippery and separate.
- Cup-shaped pasta (e.g. conchiglie, orichiette) is designed to hold sauces with larger ingredients such as mushrooms, artichokes and tomatoes.
- Cut pasta (e.g. tagliatelle, fettucine, farfalle) is best eaten with rich sauces made with cream, eggs or meat.
- Twisted pasta (e.g. fusilli, eliche, fettucine, farfalle). The curly character of these pastas means that they will trap thin sauces such as pesto, garlic, and olive oil flavoured with chilli.
- Tiny pasta shapes (alphabet letters, fillini, vermicelli) cook quickly and are ideal for adding to soups and casseroles.

TO TURN SUN-DRIED TOMATOES INTO SUN-BLUSH TOMATOES

Blush tomatoes are softer, jucier and more expensive than the sun-dried type. To get the same result, pour boiling water over sun-dried tomatoes and leave them for 20–30 minutes. Drain well and you have sun-blushed tomatoes!

TO SKIN OR BLANCH ALMONDS AND PISTACHIOS

Cover with boiling water and leave for 5 minutes, then strain. You will find that the skins slip off when you press the nuts between your thumb and forefinger.

TO SKIN HAZELNUTS

Put the nuts on a baking tray and put into a medium oven for about 5 minutes. Turn on to a clean tea towel and leave to cool. Then twist the tea towel around the nuts to make a bag. Shake and rub the nuts vigorously in the towel so that the skins rub against each other and come off.

TO REVIVE OLD NUTS

If you find some flaked almonds, walnuts or hazelnuts at the back of your cupboard, their flavour and texture can be brought back to life by gently roasting them in a dry frying pan. Be sure to swirl and shake the pan until the nuts become lightly brown, taking care not to burn them.

CORNISH PASTIES

You have no idea what you're missing if you've never tasted pasties made by a good, local baker in Cornwall. They are completely different from the pasties on offer in the rest of the country and are sold freshly baked to take home – you often get a baker's dozen (13)! Take advantage of this as they freeze well.

TO CRISP UP A DAY-OLD CRUSTY LOAF

Hold the loaf very briefly under a running cold tap. Give it a good shake and pop in a hot oven for about 10 minutes; it will be as soft and crusty as a freshly baked loaf.

TO MAKE DRY BREADCRUMBS

Don't waste your money on bought breadcrumbs, particularly bright orange ones. Dry slices of white or wholemeal bread on a flat baking sheet in the oven – just pop them in when (or immediately after) something else is cooking. Leave to dry until completely crisp, when they will snap in half easily. Cool completely and whiz in a processor or blender. Store in a polythene bag in the freezer. If you have an Aga or Rayburn leave the bread in the bottom oven until it's dry.

MALDON CRYSTAL SALT

Being born in Essex, I discovered Maldon crystal salt at an early age. It is fabulous. Made from the salty sea water in the River Blackwater, it is 98% pure and crystallises into beautiful pyramid shapes. Use it in a salt cellar, not a mill. Remember that its pronounced and salty flavour means less is required.

USING BLACK PEPPER

Always try to use freshly ground black pepper from a mill. Pepper that is pre-ground is not fresh tasting and often has other ingredients mixed in. Choose the type of mill that suits you, and if you want coarser pepper you can loosen the screw on the top of the mill or crush the seeds by hand in a pestle and mortar.

NUTMEG AT ITS BEST

Never buy ready ground nutmeg as its flavour is quickly lost. Instead, buy whole nutmegs, keep them in a screw-top jar and grate them into a dish as required. The aroma and taste is wonderful. Use the finest side on a metal grater, a micro-plane grater or a special nutmeg grater.

SPICES FOR CURRY AND OTHER ASIAN DISHES

It is better to buy whole spices from Asian stores if you have the opportunity as prices are better and the spices are fresher. Grind them yourself in a pestle and mortar or an electric coffee grinder kept for this purpose. The spices will benefit from being lightly toasted or roasted whole in a dry frying pan. Do this over a gentle heat, shaking the pan, until the spices start to smell aromatic. Cool them before grinding.

FOR GOOD-TASTING PRAWNS

Use shell-on prawns, either fresh or frozen (defrost the frozen ones overnight in the fridge). Remove the shells carefully – this is a bit fiddly but the difference in flavour is huge. If you have to use frozen shelled prawns, make sure that they are defrosted naturally. Do not put them into a colander and run under a hot tap. I can assure

SAUSAGE PASTA
(FOR 2 HUNGRY STUDENTS)

Try this cheap and easy meal.

4 fat sausages
125 g (4 oz) small dried pasta
100 g (4 oz) mushrooms,
  roughly chopped
1 medium onion, peeled and
  chopped
1-2 cloves garlic, peeled and
  chopped
1 red or green chilli, deseeded
  and chopped (optional)
6 cherry tomatoes, halved
50 g (2 oz) grated Cheddar
  cheese
salt and freshly ground black
  pepper

1. Make a slit lengthways in the sausages with either a sharp knife or scissors, remove the skins and break the sausages into small pieces.
2. Bring a large pan of salted water to the boil and cook the pasta for about 10 to 12 minutes, until it is tender.
3. Meanwhile, heat the oil in a frying pan and brown the sausage for about 5 minutes.
4. Add the onions, garlic, mushrooms and chilli and fry for 2 more minute. Add the tomatoes and season with salt and pepper.
5. Drain the pasta, then toss together with the sausage mixture and stir in the cheese.

you that this is what goes on in a lot of catering establishments, which is why the prawns taste of nothing – any flavour has been washed down the sink!

TO PEP UP MEAT DISHES
Lea and Perrins Worcestershire Sauce was invented in Worcester in 1835 by John Lea and William Perrin. Both chemists, they put together a recipe that tasted disgusting and then left it in their cellar for two years. When they tasted it again, it had matured like a fine wine. Their recipe is still a secret to this day. Try shaking it into stews, Bolognese sauce and shepherd's pie; over grilled cheese or on top of baked beans on toast. Do use the original and best brand, Lea & Perrins.

ANOTHER WAY TO ENLIVEN MEAT DISHES
A good tip - to bring a little 'zip' or intensity to the flavour of a simple meat dish, such as Bolognese or chilli con carne, is to add a teaspoon of sugar and a teaspoon of vinegar. This is particularly good if you don't have any wine to add to enrich the dish.

A QUICK WAY TO CHOP PARSLEY
This is an old trick that I learnt from a butler. Pick off all the stalks from the parsley and pop the leaves into a coffee mug so it is about three-quarters full. Use a pair of sharp kitchen scissors to snip at the parsley in the mug. It will take a few minutes but you'll end up with professional-looking chopped parsley.

TO OPEN CANS OF CORNED BEEF OR HAM

Either keep the tins in the fridge or put them in the fridge 24 hours before opening. Use a can opener to open both ends of the tin and then it is easy to push the meat out whole, ready for slicing.

USING CANNED BEANS

All beans are cooked in the can you buy them in, which makes the liquid a bit thick and unpleasant. Open the can, tip the contents into a sieve or colander and run under the cold tap to rinse well. This is particularly good for kidney beans, butter beans, mixed beans and chick peas.

TO REMOVE INSECTS FROM VEGETABLES

This is really good for vegetables straight from the garden. Fill a sink or bowl with cold water and add a couple of tablespoons of salt. Leave the vegetables or salad leaves to soak in this for about 20 minutes. The insects will sink to the bottom of the bowl and you can then clean the vegetables as normal.

TO KEEP WATERCRESS FRESH

Try to buy watercress in bunches. Loose sprigs in bags are never as good and always more expensive. To keep a bunch fresh, put it upside down in a bowl of water and keep in the fridge.

A PERFECTLY RIPE AVOCADO

Buy avocados hard when they are always cheaper and have not been squeezed by all and sundry. Ripen them on your kitchen windowsill.

They are ready when they just give as you squeeze them – their texture should feel like butter at room temperature.

TO RIPEN FRUIT AND AVOCADOS

Put them in a paper bag (or a dark drawer) with a banana. Ethylene gas is produced naturally by fruit, especially bananas, as it ripens, and it is also used commercially to ripen bananas that are picked green. Ethylene residues on the bananas will help the avocado or other fruit to ripen quickly.

TO STOP AVOCADO TURNING BROWN

Lemon juice helps to stop cut avocados turning brown. Also, if you pop the avocado stone into a bowl of guacamole or salsa, this will keep the dip fresh and green for at least 2 hours; remove the stone before serving.

SUCCULENT DRIED FRUIT FOR CAKES

If you're making a fruit cake and the fruit looks a little dry, pour boiling water over it in a bowl and leave for 30 minutes. You can add a tea bag for flavour. Drain well, remove the tea bag and proceed as normal. For Christmas or Easter cakes, fruit can be soaked overnight in brandy or rum.

TO RIPEN A PEACH OR NECTARINE

Don't buy these stone fruit in the winter, when they are overpriced, don't ripen properly and are neither sweet nor juicy. Finish part-ripe fruit on a windowsill.

TO GET MORE JUICE FROM A LEMON OR LIME

Roll the fruit on a hard surface with your hand. This makes it easier to squeeze when cut. Alternatively, pop the fruit into the microwave, on high, for 10 seconds to release the juices.

TO MAKE VANILLA SUGAR

Treat yourself to a whole vanilla pod; use a sharp knife to slit it down the middle and bury the whole pod in a large jar of caster sugar. The pod will flavour the sugar, which can be used for sweet custards and puddings. You can top up the sugar in the jar until the pod has lost its aroma.

MAKING THE MOST OF YOUR FOOD PROCESSOR

Keep your food processor on the work surface not in a cupboard, otherwise it's a palaver to get it out and plug it in for one task. If it's ready to go you'll use it more often. Your can buy a cover for it or drape over, as I do, a tea towel.

A GOOD STEAMER

Why not buy a Chinese bamboo steamer? They're cheap and good for steaming vegetables, fish and meat. You can pile one on top of the other over a large saucepan or wok to cook layers of foods.

TREAT YOURSELF TO A 'GRILLING MACHINE'

These work-top griddles (the type promoted by the American celebrity boxer) are really good. They cook food quickly and healthily and the food doesn't spit as it does on an open griddle. The smallest appliance is inexpensive and large enough to cook two chicken breasts.
● Try this succulent, juicy chicken. Let 2 chicken breasts sit for about 10 minutes in a dish with a teaspoon of olive oil, a good squeeze of lemon or lime juice, a pinch of chilli powder and a pinch of garam masala. Grill the chicken as per instructions (with the appliance), usually for about 6–7 minutes.

A RECIPE FOR COOMBE CAKE

This is a quick and deliciously moist fruit cake, a favourite during WW2, (so no metric measurements!) when some ingredients were hard to come by and tea was used for flavour.

10 oz self-raising flour
4 oz butter or margarine
$1/2$ teaspoon bicarbonate of soda
$1/2$ teaspoon baking powder
1 cup sugar
4 oz sultanas
1 cup of strong tea (no milk)

1. Rub together the fat and flour, as for pastry, add the sugar and raising agents and mix thoroughly. Add the fruit and tea, stirring well.
2. Pour into a greased loaf tin and cook for $1^{1/2}$ hours in total; $3/4$ hour at Gas 5/190°C/375°F, then reduce the heat gradually over the remaining time.
3. The cake is cooked when it is golden and firm to the touch. Cool on a wire rack. The cake keeps well in a tin, and can be served buttered.

CONVERSION TABLES

OVEN TEMPERATURES

Mark 1/4		70°C	150°F
	1/4	80	175
	1/2	100	200
	1/2	110	225
	1	130	250
	1	140	275
	2	150	300
	3	160	325
	4	180	350
	5	190	375
	6	200	400
	7	220	425
	8	230	450
	9	240	475
	9	250	500
	9	270	525

WEIGHTS

Metric	Imperial
15 g	1/2 oz
25 g	1 oz
40 g	1 1/2 oz
50 g	2 oz
100 g	3 1/2 oz
115 g	4 oz
150 g	5 oz
175 g	6 oz
200 g	7 oz
225 g	8 oz
350 g	12 oz
450 g	1 lb
500 g	1 lb 2 oz
900 g	2 lb
1k g	2 1/4 lb

VOLUMES

Metric	Imperial
150 ml	1/4 pint (5 fl oz)
200 ml	7 fl oz
300 ml	1/2 pint (10 fl oz)
425 ml	3/4 pint (15 fl oz)
575 ml	1 pint (20 fl oz)
700 ml	1 1/4 pints
1 litre	1 3/4 pints

NOTE: The measurements are equivalents, not exact conversions. Always follow either metric or imperial measures and don't mix the two. For fan ovens, reduce °C by 20°.

MICROWAVE

A microwave is not the best choice for general cooking, but it's very useful for many other things.

TO MAKE MERINGUES IN A HURRY

Take 1 medium egg white and stir in about 325 g (11 oz) sifted icing sugar, adding enough to make a pliable mixture that you are able to roll into balls about the size of a small walnut. Put 2 balls on to a plate lined with kitchen paper. Microwave on high for 30–40 seconds, until the balls are puffed up and spread out into meringues. Watch closely as they soon turn brown. These meringues are different from the regular home-made type. They are really good sandwiched together with cream and fruit: raspberries and strawberries are best as their tartness counteracts the sweet meringues.

TO REVIVE STALE CRISPS/TACOS

Sprinkle on to a plate covered with kitchen paper and cook for a 30–40 second blast on high.

MICROWAVE SETTINGS

Low	90–150 watts
Defrost	300–350 watts
Medium	450–500 watts
Medium-high	650–750 watts
High	850 watts
Jet	1000 watts

TO MAKE INSTANT CRISPY CROUTONS

Butter slices of white bread (crusts removed) and cut them into cubes. Lay in a single layer on a plate covered with greaseproof paper and microwave on high for 2 minutes, until crisp. They work just as well without the butter.

TO COOK POPPADUMS WITHOUT FRYING

Put individually on a plate covered with kitchen paper and microwave on high for 25 seconds. They will crisp up immediately.

QUICK PORRIDGE FOR ONE

Put 50 g (2 oz) porridge oats in a bowl and stir in 300 ml (1/2 pint) milk until well mixed. Microwave on high for 4–5 minutes, stirring a couple of times. Add a pinch of salt if you like and leave to stand for 2 minutes. Serve with brown sugar, golden syrup, marmalade or jam for a great start to the day.

TO SQUEEZE MORE JUICE FROM CITRUS FRUIT

Microwave on medium for about 10 seconds, cool and then squeeze as normal.

ROCK-HARD BROWN SUGAR, CRYSTALLISED HONEY/ SYRUP?

A quick blast of about 30 seconds on high will bring these back to their normal state.

TO MAKE EASY CARAMEL

In a pyrex or strong china bowl mix 4 tablespoons of sugar and 2 tablespoons of water. Microwave on high for about 3 1/2 minutes. Watch the caramel closely, and stop the microwave when it is golden as it will continue to darken for a few more moments. Be sure to use a thick cloth or oven glove to remove the hot bowl from the microwave.

TO WARM PLATES AT THE LAST MOMENT

Microwave on high for 1 minute. Make sure they don't have any metal decoration on them.

QUICK MICROWAVE LEMON OR LIME CURD

Once you've tasted this, you'll never enjoy bought curd again!

grated zest and juice of 2 lemons or 3 limes
100 g (3 1/2 oz) butter
225 g (8 oz) caster sugar
3 eggs, beaten

Mix the ingredients in a suitable bowl and microwave on high for 4–5 minutes, stirring two or three times, until the mixture has thickened. Pour into warm, clean jars and leave to cool. Cover when cold and keep in the fridge. Use within 2 weeks.

FREEZING

TO FREEZE EGGS

Egg whites and yolks can be frozen successfully and separately. For whites, make sure you label how many there are in each container. Leave whites to thaw naturally. They are ideal for making meringues: allow 50 g (2 oz) caster sugar per white and proceed as normal.

Yolks should be covered (in a container with a lid) and will keep for 4–5 weeks. Defrost and use yolks as normal in sweet and savoury dishes.

TOO MANY TOMATOES?

Remove the stalks and the tomatoes can be frozen whole in polythene bags. They can then be used in place of canned tomatoes, in a tomato or Bolognese sauce or chilli con carne. Just pop the whole frozen tomatoes into the pan at the point when you would add the canned tomatoes. Don't try to defrost them separately as they turn to mush.

A GLUT OF COOKING APPLES?

Cut the apples into quarters, core and peel them. To prevent apples turning brown whilst you are peeling them, squeeze the juice of half a lemon into a bowl of water and drop the pieces of apple into it. Drain, quickly pack the apples in polythene bags or plastic containers and freeze them. To use, put the frozen fruit in a saucepan with some sugar, add a very small amount of water and cook as normal.

TO FREEZE STRAWBERRIES

If you have a glut of strawberries and want to freeze them, lay them out individually on a tray and then pop into bags when firm. They are not the best fruits for freezing, because they break down and become mush when defrosted, but they can be used in ice cream, trifles and soufflés.

Another method is to whiz them in a food processor or blender with 2–3 tablespoons of caster sugar and then freeze. Put them through a sieve if you want to remove the fine pips.

TO FREEZE HERBS

You can freeze some herbs successfully and use them straight from frozen. All the thymes, rosemary and sage work well. Freeze on their stalks and rub or shake to remove the leaves. Herbs with softer leaves, such as tarragon and basil, do not freeze well, nor do bay leaves.

FREEZING FISH

Fish can be frozen, but not very successfully (unless you buy it already frozen). It needs to come down to freezing point more quickly than domestic freezers can manage. The best advice is to freeze fish well wrapped and for 3 weeks maximum.

TO FREEZE LEFTOVER CREAM

Freeze spare cream in an ice cube tray, and then turn out the cubes into a sealed bag for storage. The cubes are useful for enriching soups and sauces. Add frozen to hot liquid and heat gently.

TO FREEZE CRUMBLE MIX

When making fruit crumble topping, make extra and store it in a polythene bag in the freezer. It is then ready to sprinkle over fruit with no need to thaw it first. Cook in the normal way.

FROZEN SOUP AND STOCK

Freezing soups and stocks is a very good idea. I find small butter tubs and cream cartons ideal for one portion of soup. Just pop the frozen soup straight into a saucepan and heat slowly. Stock works in the same sort of containers and in ice cube trays, but be careful not to put a stock cube in a cold drink!

TO FREEZE CITRUS JUICE AND SLICES

If you have citrus juice left over when you are cooking, freeze it in ice cube trays. It is useful for drinks, dressings or all sorts of recipes that need a little juice. Try freezing lemon or lime slices in ice cubes – handy for gin and tonic.

FLOWERS IN ICE CUBES

Freezing edible flowers in ice cubes is great to do in summer, for a party. Borage (a small blue flower) looks pretty and also individual golden marigold petals.

TO MAKE ELEGANT ICE CUBES

For ice cubes as clear as a glacier mint, use water that has been boiled for at least 10 minutes. Be sure to use them within 2-3 days!

JAM AND MARMALADE TIPS

THE RIGHT SUGAR

It is always best to use Tate and Lyle sugar as it is made from imported sugar cane. British sugar is made from sugar beet and it can be very difficult to get jam and marmalade to set using sugar made from beet.

MARMALADE

It's best to use Seville oranges – bitter, marmalade oranges – from Spain. These are only available in January and February but they do make the best marmalade. They contain more pectin (for setting) than sweet oranges and also have an intense, bitter flavour.

It is possible to freeze Seville oranges: prepare them in the normal way and then freeze everything, including the pips. When you want to make some marmalade, thaw the oranges and continue with your recipe. This makes no difference at all to the finished product. Remember to note the weight of the prepared oranges so you will know how much sugar to add. If you don't have any Seville oranges, see the next tip overleaf!

NO SEVILLE ORANGES?

It is possible to make a good marmalade with equal quantities of lemons, grapefruit and regular, sweet oranges. This is known as Three Fruit Marmalade.

COOKING THE FRUIT

Always make sure that the fruit is completely cooked and soft before adding the sugar. Once sugar is added the fruit will not continue to cook and soften.

FOR FRUIT LOW IN PECTIN

Pectin is the substance in fruit that helps jams to set. Some fruit, particularly strawberries, are very low in pectin. A really good idea is to add 50 g (2 oz) of cranberries (frozen are fine) to each 450 g (1 lb) soft fruit. Cranberries are particularly rich in pectin and they enable the jam to set without impairing the flavour.

OTHER WAYS TO HELP JAM SET

Lemon juice is good, aand also the acid juice of cooked gooseberries, apples, blackcurrants or redcurrants. You can buy commercially prepared pectin, or use citric acid to boost the acid levels, but neither of these is recommended; I feel they impair the jam's flavour.

TO TEST FOR SETTING POINT

Use a small plate or saucer (bone china is best) that has been in the freezer for a good 30 minutes. The saucer will be nicely cold by the time you are ready to test whether your jam or marmalade has reached setting point. This means that when you drip some jam on to the saucer it gets cold almost immediately. You can then test it by pushing the surface with your fingertip; it should just wrinkle where it has formed a skin.

● This temperature test is useful if you have a sugar thermometer. Hold the thermometer in the boiling jam, without touching the bottom of the pan, and check the temperature. Jam sets at about 104°C (220°F).

TO DISPERSE SCUM ON COOKED JAM BEFORE POTTING

When the jam is ready to pot there is often scum on the surface. Add a very small knob of butter and stir in well. Leave for a few seconds before potting, during which time the surface of the jam will become smooth and clear. The butter won't be noticeable in the finished jam.

FILLING THE JARS

Do make sure the jars are absolutely scrupulously clean. I fill mine with boiling water just prior to potting, draining them well at the last minute. Be sure to fill the jars right to the brim because the jam does shrink back. I find it easiest to use a small ladle, but the choice is yours.

JARS AND LIDS

If you don't have jars with screw tops (save suitable ones throughout the year), you will need a circle of cellophane, parchment or greaseproof paper to cover the surface of the jam. Secure this with an elastic band or some string. Put the lids or covers on immediately.

TO LABEL POTS

Always label your jars clearly with the type of jam and the date. If, like me, you have awful writing, ask someone who has a good script to help. Home-made jams and marmalades make super gifts. Cut a largish circle of pretty material with pinking shears and this can be snapped around the lid of the jar with an elastic band for a professional finish.

HERBS FOR COOKING

The following is an A-Z of basic herbs for cooking, together with their various uses. See page 151-153 for growing herbs.

BASIL

Fresh basil, either grown as a plant or bought in a small bunch, has lovely bright-green leaves and a distinctive flavour. It is perfect with any tomato salad or sauce. Basil loses its flavour when cooked, so be sure to add it at the last moment to keep it fresh and bright. There are two schools of thought about preparation: you can either chop the leaves or tear them once they have been stripped from any tough stalks. The choice is yours.

● Try slicing an equal amount of good-tasting tomatoes and Italian mozzarella cheese. Arrange the slices on a beautiful dish. Sprinkle some basil leaves over, add a splash of good olive oil, and a little salt and freshly ground black pepper. Serve the salad at room temperature with crusty bread. This simple Italian dish is the perfect marriage of the ingredients tomatoes and basil.

BAY LEAVES

These can be used fresh, picked straight from the bush or tree. I am very fond of them and always add one or two to casseroles, stocks and soups. They can be used dry, but I prefer them fresh. Bay leaves are also useful in marinades and when baking pâtés, particularly for garnishing the surface before the pâté is cooked. A whole fresh branch or sprig can look really good on a cheeseboard.

CHIVES

These have a mild onion flavour. They can be snipped with scissors or used whole, especially as a garnish. Chives are super in green salad or potato salad. Snipped chives are good added to tuna and mayonnaise to fill brown crusty rolls. Never use dried chives.

CORIANDER

Known as cilantro in America. Buy coriander from an Asian store if possible, where you will get much larger, fresher and better value bunches that last longer. Coriander has a strong, distinct flavour that goes perfectly with

Asian and Mexican dishes. Lightly chop and sprinke it over curries and spiced dishes – a little at first to get used to the lovely flavour.

LOVAGE

This is an unusual but interesting herb with a flavour reminiscent of celery and a hint of curry. The leaves are good in salad and work well in soup with potato.

MARJORAM (OREGANO)

Often known as oregano, particularly in Greece, the wild type that grows in warm European summers is far superior in flavour to the British marjoram. It is an excellent idea to buy dried oregano when on holiday; it is a nice present for foodie friends. Marjoram and oregano are useful (dried or fresh) for rubbing into joints of meat before roasting, particularly lamb and chicken; it is also good in stuffing. Fresh marjoram is excellent with carrots; try boiling some new carrots (fresh as you can find), add a good knob of butter and a sprinkling of the freshly chopped herb.

MINT

Add mint to the boiling water for new potatoes, new carrots and peas, but do remove sprigs before serving. Mint sauce (page 51) is a classic accompaniment for roast lamb. It is also great for summer drinks and small sprigs of mint are refreshing in fruit salad.

PARSLEY

This is one of the most popular herbs. There are two types, with curly or flat leaves, and both have a wonderful bright-green colour. Curly is brighter and it is my favourite, but flat is very fashionable at the moment. Parsley has a sweet tangy flavour that enhances the taste of many foods. It can be chopped finely and used as a garnish. Never use dried parsley as it is tasteless.

● Parsley butter: this can be kept in the freezer ready to pop on top of grilled fish and meat.

Mix together a good tablespoonful of chopped parsley and 2 tablespoons of softened butter, a squeeze of lemon juice, salt and freshly ground black pepper. Roll up in greaseproof paper, into a sausage shape, and twist the ends to make a tight cylinder. Cut into slices straight from the freezer.

ROSEMARY

This is an aromatic plant with a distinctive flavour, and care must be taken not to use too much at once as it can be overpowering. Best used fresh, a sprig can be added to lamb and chicken for roasting. When roasting a leg or shoulder of lamb, halve 4–5 garlic cloves and slip them under the skin of the meat. Place a large sprig of rosemary in the pan for the joint to sit on; this will also give the gravy a good flavour. Rosemary is good finely chopped and added to fried potatoes. When very finely chopped, it can also be used in sweet biscuits and cookies.

SAGE

This herb can be pungent and must be used sparingly. Chopped, it is good with onion in stuffing for chicken and roast pork; sprigs or leaves are cooked with pork chops and joints.

● For something different try sage fritters. Dip whole leaves into a light batter (batter made with lager is good) and deep fry in sunflower oil until golden. Drain on kitchen paper and serve with mayonnaise, with some chopped parsley and lemon juice added.

TARRAGON

Be sure always to buy French tarragon as the other type, known as Russian tarragon, has no flavour and is not at all nice. It is almost the best herb ever, with a wonderful aniseed-like flavour. It is great with fish or chicken, and an important flavour in Béarnaise and Hollandaise sauces. It is used to flavour vinegar, making tarragon vinegar, which can be used for salad dressings.

● In France, chickens are rarely roasted without tarragon. Put a large bunch in the body cavity before roasting the chicken. Make a sauce using single cream, with a good amount of lightly chopped tarragon leaves stirred in at the last moment. Never use dried tarragon as it's disgusting.

THYME AND LEMON THYME

Thyme has a strong, slightly sharp flavour that can easily overpower other more delicate flavours. One of its best uses (as sprigs) is with meat and chicken cooked slowly in wine. It is also very good in stuffings and sausage dishes. Do make sure you strip the leaves from the stalks for recipes where sprigs cannot easily be picked out.

Lemon thyme is my favourite. It has a subtle, light, lemony tang that is really good with grilled chicken thighs. Make a marinade with olive oil, lemon juice, garlic, French mustard and lots of lemon thyme. Pop in the thighs for at least 2 hours or overnight. Then grill until brown and crispy.

TO KEEP CUT PARSLEY AND CORIANDER FRESH

Put in a hole-free polythene bag with a couple of tablespoons of cold water, give the bag a good shake and keep in the salad drawer of the fridge. Both herbs should keep for at least a week.

RECIPE FOR TARTARE SAUCE

It is definitely worth making your own tartare sauce. Once you have you'll never return to buying it again. It's also very quick to make.

3 tablespoons good brand thick mayonnaise
1 tablespoon chopped parsley
1 teaspoon chopped onion
1 tablespoon capers, drained
1 large or 2 small gherkins
juice of 1 lemon
salt and freshly ground black pepper

Whiz all the ingredients in a food processor (or chop finely and stir into the mayonnaise with the lemon juice). Taste to check the seasoning. It will keep for up to 2 weeks in the fridge.

CHICKEN AND GAME BIRDS

TO MAKE A SUPERMARKET CHICKEN MORE INTERESTING

For an average 1-5 kg (3 lb 5 oz) bird. If it is frozen, let it defrost for 24 hours in the fridge.

Cut an onion in half, keeping the skin as well. Place half the chopped onion, half a lemon (squeezed) and a sprig of rosemary or thyme inside the cavity. Put the chicken, onion and onion skin into a roasting tin. Rub butter or olive oil over the whole of the chicken (rather like rubbing cream into your face). Sprinkle with a little salt and freshly ground black pepper. Add about 1 cm (1/2 inch) water to the tin and cover all with foil. Roast the chicken at Gas Mark6/200°C/400°F for 1 1/2 hours. Remove the foil and cook for 20 minutes more, until the skin is brown and crisp. To check the chicken is completely cooked through, cut into the flesh between the leg and body: if the juices run clear, it is cooked.

PROPER GRAVY FOR CHICKEN, TURKEY AND ROAST MEATS

DON'T use packet/jar gravy mixes! The secret ingredients are in the bottom of the roasting tin. Pour off any excess fat, add 1 tablespoon of flour, a stock cube (optional) and 1 teaspoon marmite (optional). Using a wooden spoon or a balloon whisk, gradually add water (or the vegetable water) to the tin, over the heat, making sure all the bits are stirred in. Give it a good boil. Don't worry if it's lumpy; just pour the gravy through a sieve before serving. You can add red or white wine, cider (great with pork), a teaspoon of redcurrant jelly (good with lamb), a splash of good vinegar or a teaspoon of quince jelly (good with chicken and game). Just experiment! If you like your gravy thin, simply leave out the flour.

TO MAKE QUICK TANDOORI CHICKEN

For four people put 300 ml (1/2 pint) plain yogurt into a bowl (large enough to hold the chicken pieces). Stir in 1 tablespoon tomato purée, 1–2 crushed garlic cloves and 1–2 tablespoons curry paste; Patak's curry paste is best but the choice is yours. Cut chicken breasts into chunks or use thighs (boned, if liked) or drumsticks whole. Add them to the bowl and mix well with the yogurt. Cover and leave in the fridge overnight.

Transfer the chicken to a roasting tin or ovenproof dish, spreading all the tandoori mixture over the chicken. Cook in a preheated oven at Gas Mark 8/ 230°C/450°F, allowing 20 minutes for the breast and at least 30 minutes for drumsticks or thighs. Check that the chicken is well cooked all the way through before serving. This is also great cold.

SEASONS FOR GAME BIRDS
Pheasant
October 1st – January 31st These are often bought in a brace or pair of birds, one male (cock) and one female (hen). The female birds are more tender and tasty. An old maxim is to roast the birds up to Christmas, and casserole them afterwards because they get tougher as the season goes on.

Grouse
August 12th (known as the glorious twelfth) – December 10th Roast young birds and serve one per person. Casserole older birds.

Partridge
September 1st – January 31st There are two types of bird, the English or grey and the French red-legged partridge. English birds are considered to have a better flavour. As for pheasant, roast up to Christmas and casserole after.

HOW TO ROAST GAME
Pheasant, partridge and grouse can be dry and they should have bacon rashers wrapped over the breasts. Some people like to serve game quite pink and bloody, but it is a matter for personal taste: if you are new to game, trying it well done is probably best. To check that the birds are cooked all the way through, pierce the legs in the thick thigh meat, between the leg and body, to make sure that the juices run clear.

ROASTING TIPS
● Pop 1 peeled small whole or half a large onion inside the body cavity with a knob of butter and seasoning; a sprig of thyme is also good in the cavity.

● I always put a little water or some red wine into the roasting tin and then cover the whole tin with foil, removing it at the end of the cooking to brown the bird and bacon. Covering with foil helps to keep the meat moist and tender. Remove the foil for about the last 15–20 minutes.
● Serve bread sauce and gravy with game birds.

TO GET CRISPY ROAST POTATOES
Peel the potatoes, cut them into evenly sized pieces and boil in plenty of salted water for 10 minutes. Drain the potatoes in a colander and shake vigorously to 'ruffle' the outsides – this is what makes them crispy. Put 1 tablespoon sunflower or olive oil into a shallow baking tray, add the potatoes and shake so they are covered with oil. Cook for 1 hour in a high oven (Gas Mark 6/200°C /400°F) until crispy. You don't need a lot of fat to roast potatoes; whilst goose and duck fat make great crispy potatoes, you'll find these almost as good.

ROASTING TIMES

Pheasant Oven temperature: Gas Mark 7/220°C/425°F. Allow 20 minutes per 450 g (1 lb).
Partridge Oven temperature: Gas Mark 6/200°C/400°F. Allow 45 minutes total cooking.
Grouse Oven temperature: Gas Mark 6/200°C/400°F. Allow 35–45 minutes total cooking

ROASTING MEAT

THE BEST CUTS FOR ROASTING

Beef Boned and rolled sirloin (said to have been knighted by a king of England after he feasted on a well-cooked loin of beef) and rib, preferably on the bone (either fore rib, middle rib or wing rib). Topside can also be roasted but is often dry and needs some fat around it; it is best pot-roasted on a bed of vegetables.

Serve horseradish sauce or horseradish cream and English mustard with roast beef. Beef is excellent cold.

Lamb Leg, shoulder, and best end of neck, also known as rack of lamb. Two racks can be interlocked to make a guard of honour for roasting or they can be joined end-to-end and turned into a crown roast – your butcher can prepare these for you.

Both shoulder and leg are sold whole or in halves, and both halves are excellent. Shoulder has the sweeter, though fattier, meat and is more difficult to carve. Leg is usually more expensive but less fatty and easy to carve. A saddle of lamb is a treat for 6-8 or more, although it is expensive.

Breast of lamb is a very economical cut and is usually sold boned, stuffed and rolled, ready for roasting; it is fatty but good.

Serve mint sauce and/or redcurrant jelly with lamb. Do try to make your own mint sauce (see page 51) – it's so easy and much better than bought sauce.

Pork Loin, half legs, belly and a cut known as the hand and spring, which is the front shoulder. In my opinion, loin (on or off the bone) is superior as the meat is sweet and the crackling is marvellous. If you buy a joint on the bone, get the butcher to chine it – saw through the backbone so that you can carve more easily. Pork skin must be scored, or cut into thin strips, to help it to crisp up and so that it is easier to cut – make sure that the butcher does this. Serve apple sauce with pork: home made, never out of a jar.

TO GET GOOD PORK CRACKLING

Just before putting pork into the oven, I rub the skin with water (not oil) and then sprinkle over table salt so that it sticks to the surface. I have found that a non-fan oven makes better crackling. Occasionally the skin won't crisp; don't blame yourself: it happens.

ROASTING TIPS

Joints on the bone cook more quickly than boned meat as the bones act as heat conductors. Meat on the bone is also considered to have far more flavour. The butcher will sell meat boned and rolled but sometimes the string is too tight, which can hinder the cooking time, so check and, if necessary, it is worth re-tying it so that it is slightly looser.

50

● Beef joints smaller than 1.25 kg (3 lb) should be slow roasted as they can dry out and become tough. For stuffed joints add an extra 5 minutes per 450 g (1 lb)

● Do rest the meat for about 10 minutes or more after cooking and before carving. Then transfer it to a warm serving platter, cover with foil to keep the heat in and set it aside. This gives you time to make the gravy and the meat time to firm up and become juicy.

ROASTING TIMES

Beef on the bone Oven temperature: Gas Mark 6/ 200°C/400°F. Allow 15 minutes per 450 g (1 lb), plus 15 minutes extra. For medium-rare beef, do not cook for the extra 15 minutes.

Beef off the bone Oven temperature: Gas Mark 6/ 200°C/400°F. Allow 20 minutes per 450 g (1 lb), plus 20 minutes extra. For medium-rare beef, do not cook for the extra 20 minutes.

Lamb on the bone Oven temperature: Gas Mark 6/ 200°C/400°F. Allow 20 minutes per 450 g (1 lb) plus 20 minutes. If you like lamb slightly pink in the middle, do not cook for the extra 20 minutes.

Lamb off the bone Oven temperature: Gas Mark 6/ 200°C/400°F. Allow 25 minutes per 450 g (1 lb), plus 25 minutes extra. For slightly pink lamb, leave out the extra 25 minutes.

Pork on the bone Oven temperature: Gas Mark 6/200°C/ 400°F. Allow 25 minutes per 450 g (1 lb), plus 25 minutes extra. Pork is served cooked all the way through, never pink or rare.

Pork off the bone Oven temperature: Gas Mark 5/ 190°C/375°F. Allow 35 minutes per 450 g (1 lb) plus 35 minutes extra. Pork is served cooked all the way through, never pink or rare.

YORKSHIRE PUDDING

This mixture makes 12 individual puddings. Measure 300 ml (10 fl oz) half milk, half water. Place 100 g (4 oz) plain flour and a pinch of salt in a bowl. Add 1 egg and mix the ingredients with a wooden spoon or balloon whisk. Add a little of the milk mixture and beat well (now is the time to get rid of any lumps, when the mixture is thick). Gradually beat in the rest of the milk mixture. Pour into a jug and leave to stand for 20 minutes.

Preheat the oven to Gas Mark 7 /220°C/425°F. Pour a little dripping from the meat into non-stick patty tins and heat in the oven for about 2 minutes, until just smoking. Using a jug, pour the batter into the tins and bake for 20–25 minutes, until they are well risen, and golden brown. Have confidence – they will rise! (For gravy and roast potatoes, see pages 48 and 49.)

HOW TO MAKE MINT SAUCE

For four people use about four long or eight short stems of fresh mint. Strip the leaves and chop finely (you don't have to be too particular). Mix these together with 1 teaspoon of sugar, 1 tablespoon of cider or white wine vinegar and 2 tablespoons of water. Stir well, taste and leave to stand for at least 1 hour.

Pancake Day

PANCAKES ARE **traditional on Shrove Tuesday and a treat at any time of the year.**

This is the British type of pancake – neither the very thin crêpes that the French make, nor the thick spongy type that Americans smother in maple syrup. Nothing is nicer than these pancakes rolled up with a squeeze of lemon juice and a sprinkle of sugar.

Here are my top tips for perfect results.
1 Use a small non-stick pan.
2 Don't make the mixture too thick: a good guideline is to aim for a batter with the same texture as single cream, so add a little more or less milk to achieve this consistency.
3 Get the pan really hot before you start. Then dip a piece of kitchen paper into melted butter and use this to grease the pan lightly.
4 The first pancake does not usually work – don't worry, use it as a test for getting the temperature right. Taste it as a sample if it's just a bit out of shape or throw it away.
5 Do not feel obliged to toss pancakes; just flip them over with a small palette knife. Tossing is for experts and show-offs!
6 To keep the pancakes warm as you make them, pile them up on a plate, cover with foil and place in a warm oven.
7 To freeze the pancakes, leave on the plate, as above, until cold. Cover with cling film and freeze. Defrost on the plate naturally or in a microwave.

TO SERVE PANCAKES
The following are a few suggested fillings.
● Fresh lemon, orange or lime juice and sugar; try demerara sugar for a change.
● Marmalade with a squeeze of orange juice.
● Lemon curd mixed with Greek yogurt.
● Maple syrup. (Do make sure that you buy the imported real Canadian syrup).

PANCAKES

Makes about 10 thin pancakes
125 g (4 oz) plain flour
1 large egg
300 ml (½ pint) milk
1 tablespoon melted butter

1. Put the flour into a bowl, break in the egg and add a little of the milk. Using a small whisk or wooden spoon, gradually mix the ingredients and then beat the mixture. This is the time to beat out those lumps.

2. Gradually add the rest of the milk to make a batter with the consistency of single cream. If you have time, leave the mixture to stand for 30 minutes or so.

3. Heat and grease a small non-stick frying pan. Use either a small ladle or jug to pour in a small amount of batter. Tip the pan until the batter just covers the bottom.

4. When the pancake is set and golden underneath, flip it over to cook the other side for a few seconds. Slide it out on to a plate. Repeat with the rest of the batter.

EASTER

Easter falls between March 22 and April 25 and is the most holy of all the Christian festivals in the year. The custom of giving eggs goes back to pre-Christian times when eggs were exchanged at spring festivals as a token of renewed life.

COLOURED DECORATIVE EGGS

These eggs are for decorative purposes only, not for eating, so buy the cheapest you can get. White eggs are best for all the ideas that follow. Painted eggs look good piled up in bowls with lemons or limes and large sprigs of rosemary or fresh bay. An Easter egg hunt, outdoors, is fun if the weather is warm.

Simmer the eggs gently for 20 minutes in water with a tablespoon of vinegar added to prevent the shells from cracking; an old flannel in the bottom of the saucepan also helps.

Fill glass bowls with hot water and add 1 tablespoon vinegar to each. The acid in the vinegar helps the dye to stick to the eggs. Add food colouring and leave the eggs in the water until the shell colour is as intense as you like.

Finally, drain the eggs and leave them to dry. Then polish the shells with a little olive oil for a lovely shine.

To make pretty patterned eggs, try sticking some masking tape in a simple pattern on to the eggs before dipping them in the coloured dyes. When the egg is dry, remove the tape to reveal the interesting pattern.

TO COLOUR EGGS WITH STORECUPBOARD INGREDIENTS

You can use natural ingredients from your storecupboard. Leave the eggs in the water for different lengths of time for different shades, especially the reds. Experiment!

Yellow: Mix 3 teaspoons turmeric with water and vinegar for bright yellow eggs. This works best on eggs with white shells.

Tan or brown: Tea will give a tan or brown colour. Put loose tea or teabags in bowls, add a little boiling water and a splash of vinegar.

Purple: Soak red onion skins in water to produce a purple shade. Warm the skins and water and put in a bowl with a little vinegar.

Red Hot: cranberry and cherry juice give lovely shades of red. Alternatively, add a small cut raw beetroot to boiling water.

Orange: Heated fizzy orange gives a great orange colour.

Green: Try boiling eggs in spinach water.

SIMNEL CAKE

Originally, servant girls made this cake for Mothering Sunday in March, when they were given the day off to return home to visit their mothers. We now bake it as an Easter cake. You can use your Christmas cake recipe or buy a good fruit cake and decorate it yourself.

You will often see Simnel cake recipes made with a layer of marzipan in the middle of the cake. Don't follow this idea, it prevents the middle of the cake from cooking properly and it may sink and be rather stodgy.

TO DECORATE A SIMNEL CAKE
Make your marzipan (recipe right) or buy 450 g (1 lb) and knead it well to soften it before you start.

Turn the cake upside down if the top is not smooth enough to decorate. Spread jam or marmalade – you'll need about 1 tablespoon – on top of the cake to help the marzipan stick to it.

Mark the marzipan into thirds and use two-thirds to cover the top of the cake. Roll it out large enough to cover the top of the cake. Use a little icing sugar to prevent it from sticking and try to keep it an even thickness. Place it on the cake and press down well.

Roll the remaining marzipan into 11 balls to represent the apostles, excluding Judas. Place them evenly around the outer edge of the cake, using a little marmalade or jam to stick them in place if you wish. You can now brown the marzipan under the grill or by using a little cook's blowtorch, but be careful because it browns very quickly. This is not essential.

Wrap a yellow ribbon around the cake, then either secure it with a bright-headed pin (so you can see it to remove before

MARZIPAN

This is easy to make but if you're buying it, go for the uncoloured paste as the bright yellow type is not good (it is full of E numbers).

Makes about 450 g (1 lb), enough for a 13-cm (7 in) simnel cake

125 g (4 oz) ground almonds
125 g (4 oz) icing sugar
125 g (4 oz) caster sugar
1 large egg
squeeze of lemon juice
1 teaspoon good-quality almond extract

Mix together the almonds and sugars. Beat the egg and add half of it to the almonds with the lemon juice and almond extract. Using your hands, bring the mixture together and then add more egg as needed to bind the ingredients into a firm paste. Knead the mixture thoroughly to achieve a smooth paste.

cutting) or tie it in a large bow. Decorate the middle of the cake with small coated chocolate eggs or some Easter chicks.

ROAST SPRING LAMB
Lamb is traditional at Easter (it's at its best and it heralds the beginning of spring), although you may prefer turkey. A shoulder or leg of lamb is a good choice; if you have a good carver in the house and six or more for the meal, why not try a saddle of lamb (pages 50-51)? Order a saddle (the whole loin, from both sides of the carcass) from your butcher. Be sure to make your own mint sauce to go with it (see page 51).

Trifle or fruit salad makes a great celebratory dessert.

CHRISTMAS

There's always so much to do in the weeks leading up to Christmas, but don't panic – here are some helpful hints that could act as a checklist or give you some ideas for how to cope.

WHEN TO BUY YOUR TREE

Don't buy the tree weeks before Christmas. It will begin to look lack lustre by the big day. A week to 10 days before is fine.

TO KEEP THE NEEDLES ON YOUR TREE

Try spraying some spray starch all over the tree before you put on the decorations and lights.

MAKING YOUR TREE BRIGHT

Remember that white lights give off more light than coloured ones.

STORING DELICATE DECORATIONS

Put small tree decorations and knick-knacks in empty egg boxes. If you don't have a box for them, wrap glass balls and baubles in bubble wrap or tissue paper. An artificial wreath can be stored inside a pillowcase.

TO KEEP YOUR HOUSE SMELLING FESTIVE

Simmer a pan of orange and lemon peel to make the whole house smell fabulous. If you can get mimosa at Christmas, put some in the house, as the Italians do. It has a wonderful smell that will for ever after remind you of a happy Christmas.

TO MAKE GIFT TAGS

Save used Christmas cards and use pinking shears (if you have them) or scissors to cut out suitable pictures for tags. Check that there is no writing on the reverse, make a hole in one corner with a hole puncher and use coloured string or ribbon to attach the tags. These are good to make and sell for charity: put them into packs of 6 and wrap them in cling film.

RECYCLING WRAPPING PAPER

Try spraying lightly with starch on the reverse and press with a warm iron to perk it up.

A PATTERN FOR PLAIN BROWN PAPER

Plain brown wrapping paper can be decorated with a simple potato cut pattern. Cut a potato in half and cut a relief pattern in the top with a small sharp knife. Dip it into poster paint and press down on the paper.

WRAPPING PAPER

Stand them up in a small wastepaper bin or basket. Try using leftover roll or batch ends of wallpaper to wrap presents – this is especially good for a really large present.

RECYCLING CHRISTMAS

Apparently Christmas in the UK produces enough rubbish to fill 400,000 double-decker buses. So, start to think 'recycling'.

Cards can be recycled at local waste depots or by charity shops –

www.woodlandtrust.org.uk/recycling will give you information on who will take what. Stamps can go to Oxfam.

If you buy a tree with roots, it can be planted in the garden and brought in the following year. If not, some councils do kerbside collections or, if you have a shredder, you could compost it. If you chop up the tree into manageable pieces, you can burn it on an open fire. The needles spit a little, but it smells lovely.

Take all empty jars and bottles to be recycled and make a New Year Resolution to continue recycling for the rest of the year!

FOOD FOR THE BIG DAY

If you are organised it should be reasonably easy. Don't attempt anything you have not cooked before or try fancy recipes from magazines. Stick to the basics. It is only once every year and most people like to have all the traditional foods, including Brussels sprouts!

NEED A STARTER?

Smoked salmon is a good bet. It is easy and excellent in little sandwiches, made with brown bread, served mid-morning with champagne. Be sure to squeeze plenty of fresh lemon juice over the salmon.

Alternatively, lay out slices of smoked salmon very simply on individual plain plates with a lemon quarter and some brown bread and butter. Smoked salmon is very rich, so 50 g (2 oz) per person is enough.

CHOOSING A TURKEY

The real truth is lady turkeys are more tender. If you're buying fresh, ask your supplier for a female. If you are buying frozen you will not have a choice but, as a rule, females are smaller. The bigger the turkey the lesser the flavour and you will have more difficulty cooking it. Also, apart from cold turkey on Christmas night or Boxing Day, do you want it hanging around and eventually being thrown away?

- Opt for a turkey no bigger than 9 kg (20 lb); 5.4 kg–6.3 kg (12–14 lb) is the perfect size. Allowing 1 kg (2 lb) per person as a good guide. Make a note of the weight as you'll need it to calculate the cooking time.

- If you have a large party, buy two smaller turkeys rather than one huge one.

- Allow at least two days to thaw a frozen turkey. You may be short of space in the fridge so find a safe place outside the warm house – the garage may come in handy. Make sure the turkey is in a dish or container large enough to catch drips and keep it all well covered.

An upside-down plastic laundry basket over the top keeps nosy pets at bay.

THE STUFFING

The suggested quantities are for a 5.4–6.3 kg (12–14 lb) turkey. You could start with a packet mix and boiling water but try to whiz some fresh breadcrumbs in a food processor or blender. About 4–5 thick slices of bread of any kind will do but granary bread has a good flavour and texture. Put the crumbs in a large bowl and add 225 g (8 oz) sausagemeat. The seasoning and flavouring possibilities are endless. Try some of the following:

● Grated zest and juice of a lemon.
● 1 chopped onion or a couple of shallots, fried in a knob of butter.
● Chopped fresh thyme, sage and/or parsley .
● Chopped peeled chestnuts – fresh, canned or vacuum packed.
● Chopped dried apricots or chopped dried cranberries.

Add plenty of salt and freshly ground black pepper and a couple of beaten eggs to moisten the stuffing. Mix everything together with your hands.

TO COOK AND/OR PEEL CHESTNUTS

Use a sharp knife to cut a small slit in the rounded hump of each chestnut. Lay the slit chestnuts flat sides down on a baking tray and cook in a medium oven for about 15 minutes, until the slits have enlarged and cracked open. Leave to cool until you can easily handle them and then peel off the shells and furry lining. Eat with a little salt or use for recipes.

A GOOD VEGETARIAN OPTION

Make extra stuffing, then before adding the sausagemeat set aside a portion without sausagemeat and you have the base for a nut roast. Add extra chestnuts or chopped hazelnuts, walnuts, cashews and/or Brazil nuts. Put the mixture into a small greased loaf tin and roast it for about 40 minutes, turn out to serve. Make a meat-free gravy or sauce with vegetable stock.

TO STUFF THE TURKEY

Weigh the stuffing and make a note of it to calculate the cooking time. Remove the giblets, if there are any, and keep them to make stock for the gravy. Put the stuffing in the main cavity without packing it in too tightly. Pop a peeled and quartered onion into the other end, with a halved lemon if you like. Don't tie the legs together or truss the bird. Smother softened butter over the breast and legs using your hands. Then lay 4–5 rashers of rindless back bacon over the breast.

Extra stuffing can be rolled into balls and cooked in a separate dish or roasting tin with bacon rolls and cocktail sausages. These can be prepared the night before.

WHEN AND HOW TO STUFF?

Traditionally, the bird was stuffed the night before but because of the possibility of food poisoning, it is better to stuff it in the morning. Have everything prepared and ready, and follow the advice above on how to stuff the turkey. The stuffing can be cooked either in a small greased roasting tin or rolled into balls and roasted. You could, of course, decide not to stuff it at all, in which case pop half a lemon, a quartered onion (in its skin), a handful of parsley and a sprig of thyme into the cavity.

TO MAKE CRANBERRY SAUCE

Home-made cranberry sauce is simple and it will impress everybody because they will definitely taste the difference. Buy a packet of frozen cranberries well in advance and store them in the freezer as they often sell out.

Put the frozen cranberries in a saucepan, add 3–4 tablespoons sugar (no water) and then cook over a very low heat, stirring occasionally, for 15–20 minutes, until the cranberries burst and look cooked. Leave to cool. Grate in a little orange rind and add a squeeze of orange juice (to taste). The sauce will keep covered in the fridge for at least a week. It is really good with cold turkey.

TO PREPARE POTATOES

Make roast potatoes as this is what everybody wants. (If someone hates them, boil a few ready cleaned new potatoes.) Peel the potatoes the night before, put into a large saucepan, bowl or bucket and cover them with water. Cover and leave somewhere cold (not freezing) – in a utility area, porch, garage, garden or shed.

TO PREPARE PARSNIPS

Peel, remove their tops and bottoms and cut in half or into quarters depending on size. If they are large remove the white, woody centres. Put into cold water as for potatoes and add half a lemon to stop the parsnips turning brown.

TO PREPARE SPROUTS

Prepare these the night before as well and persuade someone in the family to help. Using a sharp knife, remove the bottom of the sprout and cut a small cross into the core. Put them in a polythene bag in a cool place or the fridge until ready to cook. There is much controversy about crossing or not: I do and my sprouts are perfect!

COOKING THE TURKEY

Add together the weight of turkey and stuffing. Cook at Gas Mark 5/180°C/350°F for 20 minutes per 450 g (1 lb), plus an extra 20 minutes. Fit the turkey snugly in a roasting tin, pour in about 2.5 cm (1 in) water (this helps keep the turkey moist and also gives a good base for the gravy), then cover the whole tray in foil. Remove the foil about 30 minutes before the end of cooking to brown the turkey.

TO MAKE GIBLET STOCK

Boil the giblets for about 30 minutes in water with 1 sliced onion, a sprig of thyme, some parsley stalks, a bay leaf, salt and pepper. Strain the stock for gravy. Your cat or dog (careful to remove all bones) will appreciate the cooled chopped up giblet meat as a Christmas treat.

IS THE TURKEY COOKED?

To check that it is cooked, pierce the area between the leg and the body of the turkey with a sharp knife. The juices should run clear and there should be no sign of blood. Transfer the turkey to a warmed serving platter, and cover with the foil. Let it rest while you make the gravy. (see page 48).

TO COOK THE VEGETABLES

Potatoes: Cut into even-sized pieces and boil for about 8-10 minutes, drain in a colander and shake or rustle them around to roughen the edges; this helps to make them crisp. Roast in a small amount of sunflower oil for 1 hour.

Parsnips: Boil these for about 5 minutes, drain well, and then roast them with or without the potatoes. Use only a little oil and they will still turn brown and crispy.

Sprouts: Bring a large saucepan of salted water to the boil. Tip in the sprouts and cook at a good rolling boil for 10–12 minutes. This is the important bit: sprouts are different sizes, so timing cannot be absolute. Take one out and test it with a sharp knife: you will know if is done, but cut it in half and have a taste if you are not sure. Drain well, put into a dish with a knob of butter and some freshly ground black pepper. Cover with foil; if you have cooked them properly they will keep warm for at least 10 minutes.

CHRISTMAS PUDDING

Though I have made them all my life I would now suggest buying one. It saves time and some are very good. Go for an upper-priced, good brand. Cook the pudding in the microwave (the instructions will be on the pack), if you like, as this avoids having yet another saucepan on top of the stove to get in your way. Not everyone likes Christmas pudding, so offer something simple, such as fresh fruit salad or raspberries in jelly as an alternative – with cream of course!

TO MAKE BRANDY BUTTER

Make your own – buying it is such a waste of money. Cream 125 g (4 oz) softened unsalted butter in a bowl or food processor. Gradually add 3 tablespoons sifted icing sugar and then 2–3 tablespoons brandy. Mix well. Use cheap brandy for cooking as its roughness makes for a stronger flavour. This can be made at least a week before and stored in the fridge; serve at room temperature.

MINCE PIES

You can make your own but there are some excellent mince pies in the shops. Try lifting the lids and popping in a small blob of brandy butter. Then warm the pies for a few minutes in the oven (not in the microwave as it makes the pastry soggy). Sift over a little icing sugar before serving.

MINCEMEAT

If you buy the mincemeat for home-made pies, add a couple of tablespoons of brandy or whisky to each jar and stir well.

COLD TURKEY

If you buy the right-sized bird you'll have enough for at least one more meal. Some say that turkey is better cold and I almost agree. Don't forget cold stuffing and serve with cranberry sauce or a good sweetish chutney. Tomatoes and a crusty loaf – or soda bread – are other good accompaniments to cold turkey.

LEFTOVER CHRISTMAS PUDDING?

If you love Christmas pudding, it is fantastic the next day, sliced and fried in a little butter until crispy on both sides and served with brandy butter. (Try not to think of the calories.)

VERY IMPORTANT

If you have been doing most or all of the cooking Make sure that you have nothing to do with the clearing away and washing up!

OTHER WINTER FESTIVALS

Hanukkah - Jewish Festival of Lights

For eight days (end December to beginning January), Hannukah marks the victory of the Maccabees over the retreating Greeks, who left behind just enough oil in a jar to burn for one day. The miracle was that it lasted for eight days. The festival is celebrated with lighted candles in the eight-branched candelabrum, or menorah. The feast includes fried foods such as doughnuts and latkes (fried grated potatoes), served with sour cream or apple sauce.

Diwali (Hindu Festival of Lights)

Celebrated for four days in October/November, in memory of King Rama and his bride Queen Sita, who were welcomed home after 14 years in exile. Diwali is the most popular Indian festival and, although the associated legends differ across south Asia, it celebrates the victory of light over dark, good over evil. Diwali means 'a row of lamps' and the point is to fill the house with as much light (candles and lamps) as possible during the festival. Sweets and dried fruits are popular foods, and fireworks are part of the festivities. Even in the frenzy of celebrations the steady burning lamp is a constant symbol of an illuminated mind.

Christingle (means Christ's light)

This festival comes from the Moravian Church, which was founded in Bohemia in 1467. The children's church service of Christingle started in 1747 and happens on the last Sunday before Christmas day. Each child carries an orange, which represents the world, with a red ribbon tied around the middle to signify Christ's passion. A lighted candle is attached for 'the light of the world' and dried fruit and sweets to represent God's created order.

Chinese New Year

A celebration that starts with the first new moon in January and continues until the full moon, 15 days later. Each year is named after a different animal. On New Years Eve a huge feast – 'surrounding the stove' or 'Weilu' – is held, . Foods eaten include whole baked or steamed fish, chicken served with its head and feet attached and uncut noodles to represent long life. On the stroke of midnight every door and window is opened to allow the old year out. New Years Day, (the 15th day and full moon) is called The Lantern Festival. It is celebrated at night with lantern displays and children carrying lamps. Firecrackers send off the old year and welcome in the new.

PARTY FOOD

Simple solutions are often the perfect answer when catering for either adults or children. For example, try some of the following suggestions for canapés or nibbles to have with drinks.

MELTED CAMEMBERT DIP
Remove a whole nicely ripe and soft camembert cheese (or a similar round cheese) from its paper and wrap it carefully in foil. Put into a small ovenproof dish to just fit the cheese, with the foil ends on top. Heat in a medium oven for about 20 minutes. Set in the centre of a plate with little biscuits, bread sticks or carrot sticks to dip. Fold back the foil and break open the cheese, which will be melted, gooey and lovely in the middle. Reheat the cheese if it begins to harden.

THINGS ON STICKS
● Halve large black grapes (preferably seedless) and thread on cocktail sticks with similar-size pieces of ripe brie sandwiched between the two halves. Make sure that the rounded sides of the grape halves are facing outwards.
● Cut mozzarella cheese (be sure to buy Italian) into 1 cm (¹/₂ in) cubes. Halve some cherry tomatoes and some stoned black olives. Thread these on cocktail sticks: olive first (rounded-side out), cheese in the middle and tomato last.
● Cut cherry tomatoes in half (Gardener's Delight if you can get them) and strip whole fresh basil

leaves from their stems. Thread tomato halves in pairs on cocktail sticks, with a basil leaf in the middle, arrange on a plate and shake over a little of the best olive oil you can afford.

VEGETABLE DIPPERS
These vegetable sticks are popular, colourful and they go with most dips. The choice is yours – the main thing is to cut the pieces as evenly as you can. This can be done in advance and they can be stored overnight in the fridge. Use a lidded plastic food container lined with wet kitchen paper on the top and bottom.
● Halve a cucumber lengthways, scoop out the seeds from the middle and cut it into sticks.
● Cut peeled carrots, celery sticks and courgettes into short sticks.
● Include small whole radishes, cherry tomatoes and baby corn.
● Remove the stalk, core and seeds from red, green and yellow peppers and cut them into sticks.

TO MAKE SPICED NUTS
These are very easy to make and so much nicer than bought ones. They are best served warm; if they are prepared ahead, reheat briefly in the microwave. Buy plain unsalted cashews and/or whole blanched almonds and fry them in a little hot sunflower oil until golden, watching them carefully as they will soon burn. Remove with a slotted spoon and drain well on kitchen paper. Sprinkle with salt and a little cayenne pepper.

PARMA HAM WRAPS

Wrap slices of Parma ham around the ends of bread sticks, leaving the other end uncovered for holding the stick. Parma ham is also good with fruit – try wrapping it around quartered fresh figs or chunks of peeled melon. Thread a cocktail stick through the ham and fruit to eat.

SANDWICH SELECTION

Though you may think they are boring, a good sandwich takes a lot of beating and there are many occasions when serving them is the perfect answer, with or without other food. Good, simple fillings work just as well as fancy ones so long as the bread is right.

SPREADS AND FILLINGS

Use softened butter, spread or mayonnaise on the bread. Mustard goes well with ham, beef or pastrami. Try the following fillings and remember to season to taste.

● Allow 1 hard-boiled egg, chopped and mixed with mayonnaise, to fill 2 sandwiches.

● A 75 g (3 oz) can of tuna, drained and mixed with mayonnaise and a splash of vinegar, will fill 3 sandwiches

● Allow about 40 g (1½ oz) cooked meat, peeled cooked prawns or smoked salmon per sandwich. If using smoked salmon, squeeze over some fresh lemon juice and a screw of black pepper.

● Do not use tomatoes – they will make the bread wet and soggy.

● Good vegetables for sandwiches include cucumber, shredded lettuce, watercress, grated carrot and mustard and cress.

HOW MANY SLICES IN A LOAF?

There are about 20 slices in a medium-sliced loaf. Thin-sliced bread is difficult to find, but some bakers will order it in advance.

HOW MANY SANDWICHES PER HEAD?

The usual portion is one and a half rounds (cut into quarters) for a normal tea with other foods or two rounds when serving on their own. Allow one round per child.

TO SLICE SANDWICHES

Slice the sandwiches when you are ready to serve them. An electric carving knife is fantastic for the job – it doesn't squash the bread or fillings. Otherwise, make sure that you use a large, sharp knife. Stack two rounds on a chopping board, cut through both into quarters (triangles) and set out the sandwiches on large plates in rows, with the cut sides up. If you are not serving them immediately cover with cling film or a damp tea towel. Remove the covers to serve and garnish with mustard and cress or chopped parsley.

CRUSTS ON OR OFF?

If it's a gentle afternoon tea and you are using cucumber or similar delicate fillings, it is best to cut the crusts off. Children also prefer crusts off. Cutting crusts off is easy with an electric knife (they are hopeless for carving meat but good for cutting sandwiches).

TO PREPARE SANDWICHES

Sandwiches can be prepared in advance. Make the fillings beforehand and store them in the fridge; egg and tuna fillings can be made the night before. Butter the whole loaf with the chosen spread and lay out the slices in two rows. Put the filling on one row and then cover with the other. Pile up the sandwiches on a tray and cover with a damp tea towel. They will stay fresh for 2 hours.

TO MAKE MULLED WINE

Pour a bottle of inexpensive red wine into a large saucepan, add 2 tablespoons of soft brown sugar, 4 cloves, half a freshly grated nutmeg and 1 cinnamon stick, snapped in two. Heat gently for 5 minutes, but do not boil. Strain, and add thin slices of orange.

TO MAKE SANGRIA

In a large jug or bowl mix together 1 bottle of cheap red wine, 1 glass of brandy, 1 glass of port, 1 large bottle of lemonade or tonic water, to taste. Leave to stand, covered, then add plenty of ice and some chopped up sweet oranges.

CHILDREN'S PARTIES

Children never eat as much food as you would expect and you can be left with mountains of sandwiches. Keep it simple and include a few healthy snacks and some non-fizzy drinks to please parents! Go for finger food, which is easy to eat, although it's also a great idea to sit everyone at a large table. Let your children choose bright paper cloths, matching napkins and paper cups. Everything can be thrown away afterwards and it means less washing up for you.

A PARTY'S NOT A PARTY WITHOUT...

● You must have balloons, streamers and hats, chosen by the birthday child, and a goodie bag for each young guest to take home (filled with birthday cake, a few sweets and a small toy). The contents don't have to be expensive but the bag should be bright and look good.
● Send out invitations and encourage replies so that you know how many to cater for.
●Put all the food (except the jelly and ice cream) on the table as children like to pick at things.
● Add a few favourite bought savoury and sweet snacks to home-made treats, with some seedless black and white grapes, picked off the stalks.
● There's nothing wrong with cheese on sticks, with a chunk of canned pineapple or half a grape. Use mild cheese, not strong.

TO MAKE SAVOURY DIPS

Soften cream cheese with milk or water to make a dipping consistency and leave some plain. Add a little tomato ketchup to

QUICK AND EASY BISCUITS

Cooking is a great activity for rainy afternoons and this is a quick recipe that your children will love to help prepare. There are some fun biscuit cutters available and children like to decorate their own biscuits.

Makes about 36

300 g (10 oz) plain flour
1 teaspoon baking powder
$^1/_2$ teaspoon bicarbonate of soda
$^1/_4$ teaspoon freshly grated
   nutmeg
125 g (4 oz) butter or margarine
175 g (6 oz) sugar
finely grated zest of 1 lemon
1 egg, beaten
To decorate
dried and/or glacé fruit
nuts
demerara sugar

1. Sift all the dry ingredients into a bowl. Using a wooden spoon, beat the fat, sugar and lemon zest together in another bowl until the mixture is soft, white and fluffy. This can be whizzed up in a food processor – but take care not to overmix.
2. Add the egg and dry ingredients alternately, beating well between each addition, until thoroughly mixed. Chill, wrapped, for at least an hour.
3. Preheat the oven to Gas Mark 5/190°C/375°F. Grease two or three baking trays. Roll out on a floured surface to about 5 mm ($^1/_4$ inch) thick. Use shaped cutters to stamp out biscuits and place on the baking trays. Decorate the cookies with currants, raisins or dried cranberries, glacé cherries, nuts or other ingredients and sprinkle with sugar (demerara sugar looks and tastes good).
4. Bake for 10–12 minutes until the biscuits are golden. Cool on a wire rack. If you don't eat them immediately, store the biscuits in an airtight tin.

another dish; snipped chives to a third dish and chopped pineapple to another dish. Provide crisps or carrot sticks to dip. I don't think other vegetables would be popular.

TINY SAUSAGE ROLLS

These go down well. Buy regular frozen sausage rolls, preferably made with puff pastry, and cut each one into two or three pieces when part-thawed. Score the tops, brush with beaten egg and bake as on the packet. Serve warm.

SAUSAGES ON STICKS

There are 32 cocktail sausages to 450 g (1 lb). If you buy chipolata sausages at 16 to 450 g (1 lb), and twist them in half yourself to make 32, they'll be almost half the price. Cut them with scissors once twisted. For ease and space, cook them in the oven in a shallow tray. Don't add any fat, just prick them. There is no need to turn them and you can pour off the excess fat when they're cooked. Serve warm, skewered on a blunt cocktail stick.

MAKE CHOCOLATE CORNFLAKE OR RICE CRISPIES

They may be old fashioned but children love them; they are easy to make and your children can help. Melt the chocolate in the microwave or in a bowl over a pan of boiling water. Plain or milk chocolate works. You can keep the crispies plain or add your child's favourite dried fruit, chopped glacé cherries and/or chopped nuts, or use a crunchy cereal with fruit and nuts. These also work well with sugar puffs, but make them small as they are very sweet.

SANDWICH SHAPES

Make sandwiches with bread as thin as you can get. Cut off the crusts and cut the sandwiches into shapes or use cookie cutters. Children may prefer white bread but the choice is yours. Small submarine rolls are good too.

THE BIRTHDAY CAKE

Most supermarkets and bakers offer wonderful cakes, so don't feel ashamed or guilty about buying one. After all, you'll be doing everything else! If you really do want to make one, why not borrow a specialist cake book from your local library rather than waste money buying a book to use once or twice a year? Do have candles – the type that don't blow out are fun. If you spill the wax you'll find all the right tips for cleaning up in this book!

FRUITY JELLIES

Remember the washing up and make them in individual paper bowls. Shades of red are best, with a little fruit in the bottom of the dishes. Tinned fruit cocktail is good. Finish with 'squirty' cream – but *you* do the squirting! For really fruity jellies, use fruit juice or the

BANANA CHOCOLATE CHIP CAKE

This is a simple cake to make with over-ripe bananas (often sold cheaply).

Makes 8 generous slices

2 large ripe bananas
100g (3 ½ oz) soft margarine
150 g (5 oz) sugar
175 g (6 oz) self-raising flour
¼ teaspoon bicarbonate of soda
1 egg
50 g (2 oz) chocolate chips

1. Preheat the oven to Gas Mark 4/ 180°C/350°F. Line a 1 kg (2 lb) loaf tin with greaseproof paper and grease it well, or a bought cake tin liner.

2. Whiz the bananas in a food processor or liquidiser until smooth. If you don't have an appliance, mash them really well with a fork.
3. Put the banana purée in a large bowl and add the margarine, sugar, flour, bicarbonate of soda and egg. Use an electric beater or wooden spoon to beat the ingredients together well. Stir in the chocolate chips and pile the mixture into the tin.
4. Cook in the oven for about 45 minutes, until the cake is well risen and golden. Cool in the tin for about 15 minutes and then transfer it to a wire rack. It may sink a little, but the flavour makes up for this.

juice from tinned fruit, instead of the cold water.

WHISKED JELLY

I ate this regularly as a child and loved it. When I was sixteen, before cookery college, I worked for a family who called it 'fluther buther' and it always seemed more exotic after that.

Dissolve a red jelly in 150 ml (¼ pint) boiling water. With an electric beater or in a food mixer, whisk a can of evaporated milk until it is thick and foamy. It might take about 20 minutes! Pour in the cooled jelly and continue beating until well mixed. Pour into bowls and chill until set – it makes about 10 small jellies or one big one.

ICE CREAM

Serve vanilla. Invest in an ice-cream scoop so you can make regular round shapes. Serve with strawberries or raspberries or chocolate sprinkles for a treat. Remember to take the ice cream out of the freezer about 10–15 minutes before serving, depending on how hot your kitchen is (soft scoop doesn't get too hard).

COLD DRINKS

Home-made lemonade is very refreshing (see page 169). You could also try cranberry juice, watered down and with a drop of honey to sweeten it. Exotic fruit juices are a treat, but water them down a little as they can be thick and strongly flavoured. Any squashes, diluted with water, are firm favourites with children. Avoid fizzy drinks for young ones.

APPLE AND GINGER FIZZ

Mix a large carton of apple juice with 1½ litres (2 pints) ginger ale. Core and slice a couple of red-skinned apples (don't peel them) and add to the drink with ice cubes and mint leaves.

MARMALADE ICE CREAM

5 tablespoons good brand or homemade dark orange marmalade
2 tablespoons fresh lemon juice
2 tablespoons soft brown sugar
600 ml (1 pint) double cream

1. Put the marmalade and lemon juice into a food processor and whiz them together until the peel is reduced to tiny specks.
2. Add the cream and sugar and whiz for another 5-10 seconds to mix well. Cover and chill in the fridge for at least an hour.
3. Pour the mixture into an ice cream maker and churn for about 20 minutes, or until it becomes ice cream.
4. Turn the ice cream into a plastic container, cover and freeze for at least 2 hours before eating.

If you don't have an ice cream maker, freeze in an uncovered container for about 2 hours, then whiz again in the food processor. Return the ice cream to the freezer as quickly as possible and cover it with a lid.

Party Games

IT IS A GOOD IDEA to have some games up your sleeve. Before the food is the best time to play so that the children work up a good appetite.

POPULAR GAMES

For younger ones there are all the old favourites: Pass the Parcel, Follow the leader and Musical bumps. As they get a little older Musical Statues works well to their favourite music, as do Pin the tail on the donkey, the eye patch on the pirate or bash the pineda (filled with sweets).

HUNT THE SWEETS

Another game for young ones. Hide sweets around the house or in the garden in summer – not in rooms you want to keep child-free! Those small chocolate Easter eggs are great, but any other wrapped sweets are good. As they arrive, give the youngsters a bag each and see who can collect the most. A prize may be given.

WASHING DAY

Tie two lengths of cord or rope between two chairs, give each team a basket of washing (hankies, T-shirts etc.) and some pegs and let them take turns to hang a piece of washing on the line. It's a race to empty the basket first

SAUSAGES!

This is a very silly game, but great fun. One child is chosen to stand in the middle and the others fire questions at him or her. For example, where do you go to school? What's your brother/sister called? How old are you? Who is your best friend? 'Sausages' is the answer that must be given every time, but the child must keep a straight

face when saying this. No giggling – the moment this happens the child is out and the questioner is in.

STRAWS AND SMARTIES

Another silly game. Have a pile of Smarties, a large bowl and a box of brightly coloured straws. The aim is for each child to use a straw to suck up a sweet and get as many Smarties into the bowl as possible. Obviously they can eat the Smarties afterwards.

PASS THE BALL

This is good outdoors or inside. Divide the children into two teams and seat them in rows facing each other. Give each team a ball, which must be placed between the ankles of the child at the head of each team. The object of the game is to pass the ball along the team using only the ankles and feet, without allowing it to touch the floor or ground. If it is dropped, the ball must go back to the beginning again. The first team to pass the ball all along the line wins.

DIY HINTS &TIPS

There is a bewildering array of DIY advice on offer these days: television series, magazine columns and radio stations seem to share the nation's obsession with home improvement. In addition there's a growing choice of DIY stores offering an impressive range of pre-fabricated and ready-to-assemble products. But there's no need to extend your overdraft to discover the satisfaction of doing it yourself. Try a few of these back-to-basics tips and you'll be able to transform your living environment along with the best of them.

Every year thousands of people are injured in falls from ladders. Safety is important and it is easy to overlook simple precautions when you're busy.

LADDERS AND GENERAL SAFETY

STORING LADDERS

Keep ladders locked away where intruders can't use them for gaining access. You can buy special wall or ceiling hooks – ideal for garage or shed. Lightweight aluminium ladders are easier to lift, carry and store.

CHECKING A LADDER

Always use a sturdy ladder. Check older wooden ladders and throw away any with rotten or deteriorating wood, loose rungs and worn-away feet. At the very least your ladder will need rubber feet – periodically check that the rubber is not worn through. You can buy new rubber feet to fit ladders to make them safer.

Replace worn ladders with lightweight metal ones with solid feet. Check the manufacturer's recommendations on where and how to use the ladders to ensure they suit your requirements.

RESTING A LADDER AGAINST A WALL

Don't rest a ladder at a wide angle too far from the wall as it will slip more easily. An angle of 70 degrees is recommended – this means 0.6 m (1 ft) away from the wall for every 1.2 m (4 ft) high.

STANDING A LADDER SAFELY

Put it on a firm, even surface, where it won't sink or topple. Test it by jumping on the first couple of rungs before climbing up. If possible, get someone to hold it at the bottom. If there's no one available, drop a sandbag over the lowest rung for a bit of weight and stability.

USING A LADDER ON SOFT GROUND

Use concrete paving slabs under a ladder when standing it on soft ground. Make sure the slabs are firmly in place. Bricks or heavy concrete blocks can be useful for keeping the feet in place. Always get someone to hold the ladder if you are not confident that it is completely stable.

TO SECURE A LADDER

As an extra precaution, if possible, lash the top of a ladder to a safe place but not to guttering or other fixtures that may pull away from a wall if the ladder slips. A part-open upstairs window may provide a suitable place for tying down a ladder, but make sure no-one moves the window.

STAYING SAFE AT HEIGHT

If you are working at height, set up a platform, such as a scaffold board, between two trestles or sets of steps. Make sure step ladders are fully opened.

WORKING BEHIND A DOOR

If your ladder is next to a door or you are working on a platform running along the length of the room behind the door, lock the door securely from the inside or put something heavy against it so it can't be opened unexpectedly or too quickly. If the door doesn't have a lock, make sure everyone in the house knows you are on a ladder behind the door.

TAKING TOOLS UP A LADDER

When climbing steps or a ladder, take care carrying tools, especially sharp items such as scissors or knives. It's a good idea to carry a bucket containing tools to hang from the top of the ladder.

PLATFORMS ON STAIRS

If you're working on a staircase try using one stepladder at the top of the stairs and an extending ladder on the lower steps. Lean the lower ladder into the riser, or upright part of the step. Rest a scaffolding plank across the rungs between the ladder and the steps at the top of the stairs to make a safe working platform.

For the lower part of the wall in a stairwell, you can place a stepladder at the foot of the stairs and rest a plank on it, with the other end resting on a step.

TO PROTECT A WALL

Wrap an old cloth around the tops of the ladder before leaning it against the wall. This protects the wall and prevents the ladder from slipping. An old pair of socks works well for this.

NON-SLIP FLOOR PROTECTION

Protect the floor with dust sheets or old sheets. Large sheets of cardboard are useful (from opened-out cartons around large domestic appliances – average cardboard boxes are too small). Don't use polythene sheets as they are slippery on the floor surface and even more dangerous when they get wet.

WORKING ON CEILINGS

Before painting or papering, prepare the ceiling by filling any cracks or gaps. Wear safety goggles. In this kind of work gravity is not your friend and bits of dust, filler, paint or wallpaper paste can get into and seriously damage your eyes.

PREPARATION

The worst part of most house-maintenance tasks is the preparation, which is a nuisance because it is usually essential. Having everything ready is important for several reasons. First and foremost, making sure the working space is clear is important for safety. Trying to work around furniture or items that have not been moved is time-consuming and frustrating, making any job slow and tedious. Having surfaces properly prepared is also essential for a good result. Always do all your preparation first before you start to decorate or do any maintenance work.

WORKING IN SAFETY

Clear the area or room of anything you don't need. Make sure there is space for ladders and that the floor is not cluttered with bits and pieces you might trip over. When working outside remove pots and wall fixings . Make sure you don't interfere with any telephone cables or other wires when leaning ladders against a wall. When you are working inside, take down soft furnishings as well as furniture.

TACKLING CEILING DECORATION

If you need to paper and/or paint the ceiling, do this first as it won't matter if you get paint on the walls. However, if you plan to use a steamer on the walls to remove old paper, do this first as it could damage the finished ceiling.

KEEPING YOURSELF CLEAN WHILST PAINTING THE CEILING

Wear a black plastic bin liner (the size that fits the dustbin). Cut holes out for your head and arms. You can cover your head with an old shower cap too.

TO STRIP OLD WALLPAPER

Dampen it with a sponge and warm water – two or three times for very heavy paper. You can add soap powder or washing up liquid to make it more effective, or a few scoops of wallpaper paste.
● For hard-to-shift or waterproof paper, first score the surface with a scraper or wire brush.
● You can hire a wallpaper steamer – this is rather like a big kettle with a vacuum cleaner attachment. It has a tank of water that heats and produces steam, which passes up a hose to a hand-held steam plate. You hold the steam plate over the paper to loosen it from the wall. This is really useful if you have a large area to strip as the paper scrapes off easily when damp and warm.

PREPARING WOOD FOR PAINTING

Fill any gaps or cracks with wood filler. Apply knotting compound to new wood, then use a primer. If existing paint is sound, don't strip it. Just clean with sugar soap and water; this will key the surface to accept new paint.

PREPARING METALWORK FOR PAINTING

Remove rust with a wire brush followed by emery paper or wet-and-dry sandpaper. Apply primer to prevent further rusting. Remove protective grease on new surfaces with white spirit.

KEEPING CLEAN AND SAFE

Make sure you are properly dressed and protected for any DIY. From head to toe:
● A shower cap protects hair when painting.
● Goggles protect eyes from dust and splashes.
● Masks protect against dust when sawing or sanding.
● Elbow and knee pads are useful when kneeling or leaning.
● Gloves may be plastic or rubber, leather or fabric to protect hands.
● Overalls or old clothes are essential.
● Sturdy shoes so that you don't slip and to protect toes.

DRAINS AND GUTTERS

Gutters and pipes can become blocked with fallen leaves or other debris and then joints in the guttering come under pressure and leak. This may lead to sagging, allowing water to gather instead of running away, and sometimes splitting. This is when water may penetrate walls, causing dampness.

DRAINS: LOOK AND LEARN

It's a good idea to have a look down drains when they are running freely to see how they work. Look at the points where down pipes enter the ground – if you have a relatively new house, they may be enclosed. If they are open, there may be grating covers where dirt gathers.

● Find the inspection cover (the big one – you may have more than one). Lift it and have a look inside. There is a chamber where water and toilet outlets converge and waste flows (hopefully) into and along a gully towards the main (public) drain. Get someone to flush a toilet or run a little water so that you can see what happens. It may not be a bed of roses but it shows what happens, so you'll know where to look if something begins to run too slowly or gurgle unpleasantly.

TO MAINTAIN DRAINS

Check and clean gutters every year. It makes sense to do this after leaf fall in autumn. Clumps of leaves and twigs are the most common blockages in down pipes. Tennis balls, dead birds and bird nests are in the top ten too.

TO CLEAN GUTTERS AND DRAINS

Before cleaning muck out of a gutter, cover the top of the down-pipe to make sure that the debris doesn't fall down the pipe. You may be able to stuff the opening with a large rag (an old shirt or something) but take care not to let it slip down the pipe. Try crumpling a plastic carrier bag in and securing it with tape in several places or tying it around the outside of the gutter.

Scoop what grit and silt you can out of the gutter and into a bucket. You can hire flexible rods but a broom handle or bamboo cane (bean pole) can work wonders. A long-handled hoe or small garden trowel is also useful.

TO FLUSH A GUTTER OR DRAIN

When you've unblocked a gutter, carefully tip in a bucket of clean water near the down pipe, flushing the whole length of the gutter. Do this three or four times.

CLEAR BUT NOT FLOWING?

If water sits in or is slow to run along the gutter when it is clear, it's because it doesn't slope towards the down pipe. The supporting brackets can be raised at the end farthest from the down pipe to ensure the guttering slopes in the right direction. This may be easy on a short and/or straight run of plastic but if the guttering is complicated or old, it may be best to seek professional help.

TO KEEP GUTTERS AND DRAINS CLEAR

Use wire or plastic covers over the tops of the guttering and pipe or fit your own wire mesh. Thin gauge plastic netting can be tied over the gutter – this is useful if you have overhanging trees.
● Check that the vent pipe or soil pipe has a little dome-shaped sieve of netting, plugged into the end of it to stop birds dropping bits down. You can buy this or make one yourself.

EMERGENCY REPAIR

Heavy duty waterproof tape or duct tape, is useful for emergency repairs to gutters – tape up cracks or joints to prevent water from seeping through.

TO UNBLOCK OUTDOOR DRAIN (SINK) TRAPS

All sorts of grot can gather on a grill-covered drain (typically outside a kitchen), including food scraps from washing-up water and leaves blown in. Hair from a bathroom outlet may gather on a grill. Cleaning obvious debris from the grill is easy – use a small trowel or piece of stick to scrape and scoop all the dirt off the grill.

If the drain is blocked under the grill (it will be full of water if it is), the U bend or trap underneath is probably blocked. General dust and silt, coarse coffee grounds and tea leaves are the sort of rubbish that build up in the trap. You may be able to push a piece of strong but flexible wire through – e.g. a length of thick but flexible electric cable.

Long-cuffed rubber gloves and a little courage is the other solution. The trap is not too low (you will be able to keep your elbow out), but it will probably smell a bit unpleasant. Flush the trap with plenty of water to clear it properly.

USING COMMERCIAL PRODUCTS

Chemicals or environmentally friendly products are available. Always follow instructions and check that the product is suitable for use in plastic drains, if appropriate. Eco-friendly products that slowly 'digest' organic matter are useful if you have time to spare and for a partially blocked trap or U bend, when they can be left overnight.

TO PINPOINT A BLOCKAGE IN A DOWN PIPE

Leaking joints on a down pipe will often indicate where it is blocked. If it's leaking near the top, try using a length of wire or an opened-out metal coat hanger to shift the blockage. Before you try anything, cover the gully at the foot of the pipe to stop debris falling into and blocking the drain.

DO YOU HAVE A SOAK-AWAY?

In older houses, if rainwater runs into a soak-away (a ditch filled with rubble, and gravel), instead of into the main drain, the householder may be entitled to a reduction in water rates.

BRICKWORK AND WALLS

DAMP PATCH ON WALL?

If there's a damp patch on an inside wall, it's worth checking the guttering first in case there's a leak, or seepage, that's causing the problem.

INSIDE OR OUT?

To determine whether dampness is caused by condensation or coming from outside, try attaching a piece of aluminium foil to the affected area. If moisture appears on the front surface, then it's condensation in the room and you should look for a better way of ventilating it. If the foil is wet on the reverse (the wall side), the damp is coming from the outside and you should call in a professional builder.

DAMP CHIMNEY BREAST?

There are a few things worth looking for from the ground. It could simply be an open pot on a little-used chimney that has lots of water running down in wet weather. Fitting a cowl, or chimney cover, could do the trick.
● Damaged, worn or missing pointing may allow water to seep in and run down the inside of the chimney.
● Flashing between the chimney and roof may be damaged, or there could be gaps where it's cut into the brickwork. If possible check in the loft for signs of dampness on the chimney stack.

TO RE-POINT WALLS

Old, damaged or crumbling pointing should be replaced. Pointing protects the walls from water and weather erosion. You can buy raking-out tools to scrape out defective or crumbling mortar and the procedure is quick and reasonably effortless. The problem is trying to match the colour of new pointing with old. Patching up is a good idea to prevent deterioration, but if it's in an obvious place where it won't match up, plan to repoint the whole wall, or patch it up and then budget for a professional job later.
● Ready-mixed mortar is easiest.
● Before pointing you should brush the joint with water to prevent the dry bricks from sucking out water from the mortar and making it crack or crumble.
● Tackle the vertical joints first and then the horizontal ones.
● In very hot weather spray the joints to keep them damp and soft for a few days so the heat doesn't cause them to crumble and crack.

TO MATCH THE COLOUR OF EXISTING POINTING

Try different proportions of cement, sand and lime to get the best colour and consistency. Make a note of the mix used. Then re-point a small area and leave it to dry for a couple of weeks before comparing new and old pointing.

DOORS AND WINDOWS

TO STOP A DOOR SQUEAKING

Use a lubricant, such as WD40 or a little three-in-one oil, to grease the moving parts of the hinge. Move the door back and forth a few times to work the oil in, and then wipe away the excess.

TO SORT OUT A STICKING DOOR

Whether at the top or bottom, the solution for internal doors is to plane a little off. Remove the door and secure it in a portable workbench. Remember you will have to plane against the grain at either edge, so start on the outside and work in. If the door sticks at the sides the most likely cause is paint build-up. Strip the edge of the door, the frame or both, depending on the severity of the problem, then re-paint.

You need strength and another person ro remove heavy doors, so consider getting professional help. If an external door sticks at the bottom this may be due to moisture being absorbed in wet weather. Take the door off its hinges and dry thoroughly, using a hot air gun if necessary. Then plane the edge as described above. Finally, prime and paint the edge to prevent further absorption.

LATCHES NOT ENGAGING?

This often happens on new doors that sag a little after they have been fitted and used. Many types of new door have adjustment mechanisms incorporated into their hinges, so check with the supplier or person who fitted the door. If the problem cannot be solved by adjustment, the aperture into which the bolt fits as the door clicks shut can be enlarged (usually downwards) with a metal file and/or junior hacksaw.

TO LIFT SAGGING DOORS

If the bottom of an older door rubs on the floor or the bolt catches on the lock plate, it is often because of loose hinges. Open the door halfway and pull the handle firmly upwards to see if the hinges move. If they do you may be able to tighten the screws. If the holes are too big, you might be able to pack them with pieces of matchstick and then do up the screws.

Alternatively, try bigger gauge screws. If the holes in the hinges won't take bigger screws, fit new hinges of the same size but with bigger countersunk apertures.

HINGE-BOUND DOORS

When doors are hard to keep shut and spring open easily, this is often because hinges are set too deep in the door or frame. You may be able to see which hinges are too far below the recesses. Raise them by putting strips of cardboard underneath.

Occasionally screw heads may protrude and stop hinges from

closing properly. You may have to fit smaller screws that sit well into the hinges.

TO LOOSEN STICKING LOCKS

Squirt WD40 into the latch, bolt holes and keyhole using the straw-type applicator.

If squirting in a little lubricant doesn't work, remove the lock, take off one of the sides of the case and note the position of the components in case they are disturbed and need reassembling. Lightly grease all moving parts.

If you have a Yale-type lock, use a dry powder or graphite-based lubricant, as grease attracts grit.

TO REDUCE WINDOW GAPS

Gaps between wall and window frames are the biggest cause of rot. Occasionally you may notice damp patches on the inside wall near the window. Seal cracks of up to 1 cm ($\frac{1}{2}$ inch) wide with a frame sealant (the type of filler you use in a squeeze gun). Follow the manufacturer's instructions for drying and finishing.

If the gap is bigger than 1 cm ($\frac{1}{2}$ inch), start with mortar (ready mixed is easiest) or look for an exterior filler designed for use in larger cracks (these usually have to be built up in stages). Begin by dampening the crack with water using a plant sprayer or brush. Apply the mortar level with the brickwork and in two or three days, when it has hardened, seal it with frame sealant as above.

If you have big or irregular gaps or hidden gaps that are difficult to access, go for expanding foam filler. It will stick to most building materials. Inject it into any space and it will expand to fill. Once it has hardened you can paint, cut, sand or plaster it. Expanding filler is also rot proof and heat, cold and water resistant.

Be careful if you have not used expanding filler before and apply a little at first – it expands hugely!

TO FIX STICKY WINDOWS

Sticking wooden windows can often be helped by rubbing a candle repeatedly over the touching surfaces. If the sticking continues, the real issue is why it is happening. Often, especially on sash windows, it's a build up of paint. The answer is to strip off all the old paint, then sand down and redecorate.

If the problem is caused by woodwork swollen from absorbing damp, the only way to solve it is to strip and sand or plane down the woodwork when it has dried out. Decorate thoroughly to stop damp from being absorbed. The source of damp may need sorting out – rotten or poor fitting frames may need replacing. If there is no obvious reason and your DIY effort is unsuccessful, take professional advice.

WHICH WINDOW LOCKS?

Window locks are designed to prevent intruders from breaking the glass and opening the catch from the outside. Some locks will immobilize the catch or stay-arm, but most work by locking the frames together. Different locks are designed for different windows: surface-mounted locks are easiest on casement windows.

You can fit more than one lock on each window for added security or if the window is very large.

● Sash windows are best fitted with dual screw locks, often one on each side. They consist of bolts that go through a barrel in the inner frame into the outer frame.

● Surface-fitted bolts are also popular on sash windows. These are simply obstructions on the outer frame which limit the extent to which the window will open. They are also useful for preventing small children leaping from bedroom windows.

● Modern casement windows usually have lockable handles. You can buy these, either left- or right-handed, from DIY shops and hardware suppliers.

● Metal windows often have stay bolts to stop the arm moving, but surface-mounted locks are available with self-tapping screws to fit into metal frames.

TO KEEP KEYS SAFE

If you have key-operated locks and keep the keys on the windowsill, it's not much of a challenge for the casual burglar. Decide where to keep the keys, then make sure everyone knows where they are in the event of an emergency. For the same reason, the keys should be kept in the rooms, not in a pot somewhere else in the house.

HOME ELECTRICS

EMERGENCIES

If your electricity fails, you will need to check to see if neighbouring houses have lost their power too. If they have, there will be a number in your telephone book under 'electricity' for reporting the failure.

If it's just you, then the chances are a fuse may have blown. Fuses are a safety mechanism to prevent serious electrical malfunction. You may have plugged in an appliance which has a fault and which has blown the fuse. In this case, unplug the offending article and don't plug it in again. Meanwhile, attend to the fuse.

When one fuse fails in a house circuit, all the lights and appliances connected to that circuit will fail too.

CHANGING A HOUSE CIRCUIT FUSE

Fuse boxes, or consumer units as they are now known, are often under the stairs along with the electricity meter.

When you first move to your house it is very important to locate the fuse box and note the type of fuses it contains. You will then be able to keep the right sort of repair equipment next to the consumer unit.

First identify the electricity switch and turn it to the OFF position. Keep a torch permanently in a place where you can locate it in a power cut. Near the fuse box is a good idea.

Depending on the age of your electrics you may find one of these types of fuse.

● **Circuit Breakers**

These fuses don't have to be replaced, (so consequently they're the best type to have), but they do have to be reset. It couldn't be easier: a red button pops out when the circuit is broken, or a switch will be down in the 'off' position, when you look at it.

2 Push the red button in, or put the switch back to 'up', then turn the electricity back on.

● **Traditional Fuses**

1 Pull the fuses out one by one to check which one has broken; the wire will be severed.

2 Undo both small screws at the ends of the fuse and remove any old wire. Cut a length of new wire of the same rating.

3 Thread the wire across the fuse, winding the ends around the screws. Screw them up tightly.

4 Trim any excess wire, then replace the fuse and turn the electricity back on.

You can buy fuse wire of different ratings for different circuits in hardware and DIY stores: 5 amp wire is generally used for lighting circuits, 15 amp for single appliance circuits up to 3 kilowatts, and 30 amp wire is for socket circuits and cookers up to 13 kilowatts.

● **Cartridge Fuses**

1 Pull out each fuse holder in turn, the failed one will be blackened.

2 Unscrew the cartridge holder and lever out the old fuse. Replace it with a new one of the same rating. Screw the cartridge back together and switch on.

FITTING PLUGS

Today all new appliances come with moulded plugs attached to cables. You can get to the fuse at the back through a small window, but you won't be able to open the plug itself.

Many of us will still have some appliances that have the old-style detachable plugs. If an appliance has caused a fuse to blow, you will probably need to open up the plug and check to see where the fault is. You may find the fuse is discoloured at either end where it has blown. Make sure you replace it with the same rating fuse: the most common are .3 or 13 amp; 5 amp fuses are no longer in use.

Better still, before you fit the fuse, check that the right fuse was used in the first place.

● 3 amp fuses are for appliances up to 700 watts; you will find the wattage on a rating plate on your appliance.

● 13 amp fuses are suitable for appliances between 700 and 3000 watts. Kitchen and household appliances such as kettles, toasters, dishwashers, vacuum cleaners and irons come into this category.

WIRING A PLUG

Some small appliances are not earthed, which means that they don't have a green/yellow earth wire, only live and neutral. In this case, leave the earth terminal empty.

1 Unscrew the plug cover and cord grip. Loosen the small screws or pins which hold the wires in place.

2 Check that the wire from the appliance is in good condition - not frayed or worn.

Cut off the end of the wire neatly. Then slit the outer covering about 3–5 cm (1–2 ins) to reveal the two or three thinner wires inside. Take care not to damage the inner wire coverings.

3 Carefully strip the insulation from each of the inner wires to reveal about 1 cm (½ in) of bare wire (make sure that you do not cut through the bare wire or make it ragged) Twist the bare wire ends together.

4 Thread the whole wire under the cord grip, then take each of the core wires to their respective terminals, pins or screws, and secure them tightly.

You will find three different coloured wires: Brown is Live; Blue is Neutral; Green/Green-yellow is Earth

5 Press the core wires neatly into place, and screw the plastic cord gripper down tightly. This is important as the attachments to the terminals are not strong enough to hold the wire in place on their own.

6 Replace the plug cover, and screw together securely

CHANGING LIGHT BULBS

Switch off the light or lamp and let the old bulb cool down, then remove it. Twist anti-clockwise for a bayonet type, or unscrew anti-clockwise for a screw-on bulb.

Insert a new bulb, but never force it in or screw it too tightly.

FLUORESCENT LIGHTS

If the light is flickering it may be the 'starter' that is at fault, not the whole tube. You could buy a replacement starter first, then you will know what it looks like and see where it is on the light fitting.

Turn off the electricity, and you will be able to either unscrew or pull out the old starter and replace it with a new one. If the light still flickers, you'll need a new tube.

REPLACE A FLUORESCENT TUBE

1 Switch off the electricity

2 Pull off the spring-loaded bracket at one end of the tube to release the mechanism that holds the tube in place.

3 When one end of the tube is free, pull it out to release the other end (it's a good idea to get someone to help).

4 Fit the new tube by reversing the above steps. Turn the electricity back on.

BASIC PLUMBING

LEAKING WATER

If water is pouring from the roof space (where you will generally find the cold water tank) you need to turn off the main stopcock. Turn it clockwise. Good places to find the stopcock are under the kitchen sink or in a scullery area. Meanwhile get someone to put buckets under the leak or leaks. If you can't turn off the stopcock, go to the tank, find the ball-valve arm and tie it up to stop the automatic refilling of the cistern.

If you live in an old house you may have to turn off the stopcock from outside the house. As with electricity meters you need to know where the stopcock is as soon as you move in. If you have difficulty locating it, ask your neighbours for advice.

If the water is coming into contact with the electrical wiring you may have to turn off the electricity supply as well.

Once the water tank is empty and you've cleaned up the worst of the mess, call a plumber.

FROZEN PIPES

First, try to locate where the pipe is actually frozen. If most of the system is working, with just one tap not receiving water, it will be easy to find the frozen area, particularly if the pipe is on an outside wall.

When you've found the likely area, check as far as possible for any damage – water expands as it freezes and ice can crack pipes, particularly old and fragile metal ones (plastic drainpipes are best). It can also push the pipes out of connecting joints and fittings.

Turn off the water at the stop cock/mains and place a bucket under the pipe. If you think that the water flow to the central heating or water heater is affected turn it off as well.

Warm the frozen area as closely as you can with hot water bottles, a fan heater, even a hair dryer. Do not apply fierce heat directly to a section of pipe as this may cause more trouble. If none of this works, call a plumber.

LAGGING PIPES

To prevent any of the above problems, all pipes should lagged to stop the loss of heat, particularly those near or on outside walls, in the attic, or in outside toilets. Tubular pipe lagging is the easiest, available in various diameters to fit all sizes, it comes ready slit, lengthways, for easy fitting. Thick pads of newspaper and bubble wrap make good short-term lagging.

HOT WATER TANKS

Some tanks come with ready-made jackets to prevent heat loss. Alternatively you should buy a special jacket, which is as good a fit as possible. A well-lagged tank prevents heat loss, reduces fuel consumption and keeps stored water hot for longer after the boiler has been turned off.

UNBLOCKING A SINK

All sorts of things can block your kitchen sink; be careful about pouring down liquid fat or oil, and if you do, make sure you follow it with a strong solution of hot water and washing soda. Doing this about once every two weeks will keep a kitchen sink happy.

● Bail out any excess water in the sink. Clear away all the debris from the plug hole with an old toothbrush or skewer.

● Caustic soda (available at the ironmongers or DIY store) can clear a severe build-up, but always take care when using it, and make sure you follow the manufacturers instructions to the letter.

● A sink plunger can also help, place it over the plug hole and pump up and down as vigorously as you can.

If all of this fails, you will need to remove the 'trap' under the sink, which could be one of the following:

- U-shaped metal bend
- bottle trap, usually plastic
- plastic P trap or S trap

Make sure you clear everything out from under the sink, then put a bucket under the trap (or a large bowl if a bucket won't fit)

You will see which sort of trap you have, and you'll be able to unscrew either a nut facing downwards, or two plastic nuts, which will enable you to remove a section of pipe.

The dirty water will come flooding out, but if not, use an opened-out metal coat hanger to poke upwards towards the plughole; this should shift the blockage.

Screw everything back together as tightly as you can, and then run some boiling water down the sink, followed by hot water and washing soda. When you've done this once it will make you think twice about what you put down your sink, as it's not a pleasant job!

Bath traps can be treated in the same way, though they are much more difficult to get at.

MENDING A DRIPPING TAP

A dripping tap is usually caused by a worn washer. It can be the most annoying and frustrating thing, apart from the loss of water that you're paying for.

There are two main types of tap: the pillar tap, traditional in shape, and the 'supatap', which is more chunky and contemporary.

- **Pillar Tap**

1. Turn off the water supply at the nearest point, and open the tap to drain away any water in the pipe. Put in the plug so you don't loose any bits and pieces down the hole.

2 Loosen the screw which secures the tap handle, either on the top or side, then lift the handle off.

3 Use an adjustable spanner to loosen the tap cover, (protect the cover by placing a cloth over it) then undo the large nut inside.

4 Lift out the mechanism and you'll see a spindle inside with a washer on the end. The washer is usually held in place by a small nut. Remove the nut, then replace the washer, reassemble the tap and turn the water back on.

- **Supatap**

This type is easier, as the water doesn't need to be turned off. Put in the plug so you don't loose any bits and pieces down the hole.

1 Loosen the retaining nut on the tap using an adjustable spanner. Hold the nut with one hand and unscrew the tap nozzle. Water will gush out until the nozzle is completely removed.

2 Hit the nozzle firmly and the jumper or anti-splash device will drop out. Prise out the jumper and washer unit and replace the washer, then reassemble the tap.

3 If all of this sounds too complicated, get in a professional, though it would be best if you had more than a dripping tap for him/her to attend too.

REPLACING A FAULTY BALL VALVE IN THE TOILET CISTERN

Sometimes the water flow into the toilet cistern does not stop after a minute or so. This is usually caused by a faulty ball valve. Take the top off the cistern. If the ball (or float) has deflated, then it needs replacing. This is a simple job of unscrewing the old one and screwing in a new one., which you can get at DIY stores.

If this is not the problem, then it is probably a job for a professional plumber.

PAINTING

BRUSH TIPS

● Buy decent brushes, treat them well, using the following hints and tips, and they will last. Synthetic brushes are easy to clean and don't shed bristles.

● As a rule, you'll need 1 cm ($^1/_2$ inch), 2.5 cm (1 inch) and 5 cm (2 inch) brushes for woodwork and a 10–15 cm (4–6 inch) brush for walls and ceilings. An angled 1.5 cm (3/4 in) brush is useful for window frames.

● Brushes with handles at right angles (often called crevice or radiator brushes) make it easier paint awkward places, for example behind radiators and pipes.

ROLLER TIPS

Rollers cover large areas quickly and are great for water-based paints, but it's difficult to remove oil-based paint from a roller, so it's best to use brushes instead.

● Foam rollers are cheapest and fine for average jobs; mohair rollers are great for fine finishes, especially on doors.

● Thick-pile rollers (lambs wool or nylon) are good for textured surfaces, for example to cover crevices and imperfections. Heavy duty nylon rollers can be used on stippled or pebbledash walls.

● You can get small rollers on long handles to get behind radiators –

they are also useful for narrow areas of wall (for example boxing around pipes) or to get into curved ceiling edges.

● Extending roller handles are useful for painting walls without using steps and for stairwells or high areas that are out of reach.

TO CLEAN A BRUSH

Remove oil-based paints with white spirit. Emulsion and acrylic paints can be rinsed off with water then cleaned with a little washing-up liquid. Rinse well before wiping with a lint-free cloth or shaking out and leaving to dry.

TO CLEAN A ROLLER

Run it over the ridged part of the tray and then repeatedly work the roller over sheets of paper to remove as much paint as possible. Remove the sleeve and wash under the tap as above, using your hands to squeeze out the paint.

STORING BRUSHES

The best way to store brushes and rollers is wrapped in brown paper or a lint-free cloth. Make sure they are thoroughly dry first and don't leave them in a damp place.

SELECTING PAINT

There is an incredible choice of paint – smooth or textured, to disguise uneven surfaces, to cover in one coat, water-resistant, kitchen friendly and so on. This is before you even consider colour or whether you want glitter or sparkle. Before you start looking at the aesthetics, consider the practicalities. The following are a few points to think about first. There are types of paint for all these requirements. Narrow the choice down to suitable types first, then consider the different qualities available and, finally, pick up the relevant colour charts to start on the aesthetics.

- Inside or out: is it brick, concrete, plaster or wood?
- Type of wall or surface: is it smooth or rough, even or uneven? Is it new plaster, and how good are you at painting over paper?
- What colour are you covering?
- Use and level of wear: are you painting a kitchen or bathroom, bedroom or hallway, and how long do you expect the paint to last? Do you want it to be long lasting or for a short time (for example in a child's room)?

TO ENSURE COMPATABILITY

If you are applying more than one coat of different finishes, the paints must be compatible. For example, you may be using a primer, an undercoat and a finishing coat. Follow the manufacturer's instructions and use compatible products, otherwise the paint could end up bubbling and flaking.

SELECTING SPECIALIST PAINT

There are paints that contain fire-resistant additives, ideal for painting combustible polystyrene tiles and wood surfaces; anti-damp paint; insulating paint to reduce heat loss; radiator enamel, which stays white despite exposure to heat, and various floor paints for wood or concrete. There are paints for ceramic tiles, plastic surfaces or rust-treated metal. You'll find non-toxic, high-gloss paints for nursery furniture or toys. There is an amazing choice and it is worth looking at specialist suppliers as well as larger DIY stores if you have a specific task or problem.

WHEN TO USE UNDERCOAT

Undercoat is used to prepare specific surfaces (such as bare wood) for paint. It may form a seal between a material that is likely to react badly with a paint. It may help the paint to stick, especially oil-based paints. Alternatively, it may be an effective product for covering up strong colour. Always check the manufacturer's instructions when using an unusual paint product as it may need a special undercoat.

TO DRIP OR NOT TO DRIP

The majority of paint is non-drip. Cheap paint – typically the white stuff sold in huge tubs – tends to be thinner, both in terms of dripping and coverage.

TO DECIDE ON A COLOUR

When painting a room in a single colour, choose a shade lighter than you think you want because the paint tends to look darker when it is actually on the walls, especially when the entire room is the same colour. Buy sample pots and paint patches on the wall to see what the colour looks like – leave it for a few days or a couple of weeks to see if you really like the colour.

TO PREVENT WHITE PAINT FROM YELLOWING

Add several drops of black paint to every litre of white paint and stir really well before using.

TO MAKE CHEAP BESPOKE COLOURS

Look out for an inexpensive paint mixing tool – rather like a long food mixer blade – to fit in an electric drill. This mixes paint well. Instead of buying an expensive 'shade' of white or having a colour mixed to your requirements, buy a small pot of strongly coloured paint and use a little to tint a large pot of white paint. Sample pots are ideal for this. Mix enough to finish painting the room otherwise you may not get the colour right second time around.

PAINTING NEW PLASTER

Use standard emulsion and thin it with water. Add an equal quantity or water or two-thirds water to one-third paint for the first coat. If you paint ordinary strength paint straight on to new plaster it will peel off.

TO STIR OR NOT TO STIR?

Check that the paint should be stirred before diving in with vigour; many non-drip paints should be stirred only very lightly or not at all. A wooden spoon is ideal – keep an old one specially for this purpose. Old paint that has separated should be stirred, but remember to remove any skin carefully first.

LOADING A BRUSH

You'll need less paint on the brush if it is thin and runny. Non-drip paints should be loaded fairly generously on a brush or roller. Also, when covering textured surfaces you'll need more paint than usual.

TO DEVELOP A GOOD BRUSHING TECHNIQUE

With emulsion, work the paint in all directions, being especially careful not to apply it too thickly. Finish, or 'lay off' to use the technical term, either with vertical strokes or in a criss-cross pattern.

With an oil-based paint (gloss) begin by painting three vertical stripes with a narrow gap between each, a little less than the width of the brush. Then, without reloading with paint, brush across picking up the excess paint to fill the gaps. Go over the whole section with vertical strokes. Paint a similar section directly underneath, taking care to blend into the area previously painted, and not to allow build-up where the sections meet.

TO PAINT AWKWARD AREAS A ROLLER WON'T REACH

Use a brush to paint corners, edges and other areas that a roller won't reach before using the roller to paint a large area of wall. This is known as 'cutting in'. Start with a few strokes at right angles to the edge or corner and then, without re-loading, brush in a smooth vertical movement over the horizontal strokes.

LOADING A ROLLER
Dip the roller into the well of the tray and then draw it back along the ridged part to remove excess and help an even spread.

TO ROLL EVENLY
Be careful not to press too hard on a roller or you'll have ridges of paint squeezed out of the end of the roller. Paint diagonally and then finish off as the roller dries up by painting lightly with smooth vertical strokes.

TO KEEP A BRUSH OF PAINT FRESH
Wrap it tightly in kitchen foil, cling film or a plastic bag secured with an elastic band. Leave in water if you are letting it stand for more than an hour or so – for example, if you leave it overnight.

TO KEEP A BRUSH OF GLOSS PAINT FRESH
Gloss paint can be left for longer in a jar of water. Drill a narrow hole through the handle and put a length of wire through it to suspend it over the jar. Make sure the bristles are submerged and not touching the bottom of the jar, or they will become misshapen.

TO STOP THE LID ON THE TIN FROM STICKING
Wipe the rim and lid of the tin clean when you have finished painting and then rub a little Vaseline around the rim of the lid before putting it on.

TO STOP SKIN FORMING ON PAINT IN A TIN
Make sure the lid is firmly in place and store the tin upside down.

TO PAINT A CEILING
Paint the ceiling first to avoid drips and splashes falling on your freshly painted walls. You can use an extension handle on a roller but you will still need a ladder and brush for the awkward bits.

TO PAINT EXPANDED POLYSTYRENE CEILING TILES
Use emulsion paint. These should not be painted with gloss as the combination creates a fire hazard. If you are going to cover the ceiling with tile,s paint them before putting them up, even if you have to go over them lightly once they are in place.

TO PAINT LINING PAPER
Lining paper is a great surface to paint on. Use at least two coats of emulsion and don't worry if small bubbles appear on the paper – they'll disappear as the paint dries.

TO PAINT OVER WALLPAPER
Painting over old wallpaper can give good results. If the paper starts to bubble or flake, strip it entirely. Paint applied over relief or textured papers needs to be worked in harder with a brush or a shaggy roller. If you need to cover a vinyl paper, use vinyl emulsion.

TO PAINT OVER GLOSS
You can paint new emulsion over old (but wash it down thoroughly first). If you have to paint over gloss paint, rub it down with fine

wet-and-dry sandpaper, dampened with a little clean water, to destroy the glaze.

PERFECT WOODWORK

Use knotting compound on knots, which may ooze resin from new wood. Apply primer and leave to dry. Then rub lightly with fine grade sandpaper to remove any rough bits. Next, give it one or two coats of undercoat, depending on how dark the surface is. Once dry, rub the surface with sandpaper and remove any dust or bits with a large, soft dusting brush. Finally wipe the surface with a dampened lint-free cloth.

Your surface should now be certifiably dust-free and ready for the top coat. Gloss is best for wood as it is hard wearing and easier to clean than emulsion.

TO PAINT DOORS

Paint doors first and then their frames. This way you can make sure the door is opened to best advantage before you begin. Cover any splashes on the frame later.
● Use different-sized brushes for separate bits and don't put too much paint on the mouldings as this will leave drips and lumps.

TO PAINT WINDOW FRAMES

Use a paint shield or masking tape to protect the glass. Don't leave tape on the glass for too long after the paint has dried, or it may be difficult to remove.
● A small-angled cutting-in brush works best around narrow frames. Allow paint to cover a couple of millimetres of the glass to help seal the gap.

● If you get gloss paint on glass, use a rag and white spirit to rub it off. Once dried, use a razor blade, or you can buy special scrapers.

TO PAINT CASEMENT FRAMES

Open the window. Use a small brush to paint the inner bits, then paint the horizontal sections, top and bottom. Lastly, paint the verticals to left and right.

TO PAINT SASH WINDOWS

The problem is getting at all the different bits of a sash. Try reversing the windows – pull the top sash up and the bottom one down as far as feels comfortable. Be careful – if you jerk the two parts in opposite directions too sharply they may stick in that position. Paint all the accessible sections and then move them back until almost closed and continue to paint. Paint very lightly behind sash cords to avoid getting paint on them. When the paint is thoroughly dry, rub a candle along the moving parts so that they work easily.

TO PAINT METAL WINDOWS

Metal windows are generally made to fit more tightly than wood frames, so strip layers of old paint away first, otherwise too many layers of paint will make them difficult to shut. Chemical stripper is probably best for this.

TO PAINT SKIRTING BOARDS

Ideally, take up fitted carpets before painting skirting boards as they're almost impossible to protect. The gap beneath a skirting board is full of the sort of dust you don't want in your paint, so shield your brush from the bare floor with a length of card as you paint. Use a 5–7.5 cm (2–3 inch) brush and work lengthways.

TO PAINT RADIATORS

Let radiators and pipes cool before you paint them, and clean surfaces thoroughly. It is best to use special radiator paint if you want the radiators white, as ordinary white paint yellows when exposed to heat.

New radiators and pipes can be painted with gloss, but go easy to prevent runs, and paint a second thin coat only when the first is dry. If the radiator or pipe is already painted you can simply add a fresh coat or two to cover up a dark or old colour. Don't paint over valves on radiators or pipes as they have to turn easily.

TO PAINT PICTURE RAILS

Paint several thin coats to avoid having drips and lumps in any intricate details of the rails. Don't forget to protect carpets with dust sheets, and paint the picture rail before you hang wallpaper.

EXTERIOR PAINTING

You really need to redo exterior paintwork every four to five years to keep it in good condition. Here are a few basic tips on when and how to tackle outdoor painting.

● Paint doesn't take well on a damp surface, so wait until a dry spell of weather, allowing a couple of days or more for surfaces to dry out properly first.

● Windy conditions will mean dust and dirt on new paintwork.

● No matter how keen you are, don't start painting until after the morning dew has evaporated and stop a couple of hours before the sun goes down, so that the paint has time to dry before the evening dew settles.

● It's a good idea to follow the sun around the house, starting on the east side and moving south, north and finally west. This allows the surface to dry out more quickly. However, when you're using white paint, bright sun can make it hard to tell which bits have been painted.

TO PAINT A ROUGH WALL

A rough-textured wall will need more paint than a smooth surface.

WHERE TO START?

If you're painting the whole house, start at the top and work down.

TO ENSURE EVEN COLOUR

It's a good idea to buy all the paint from the same numbered batch as the colour may vary between batches. Check the batch number on the bottom of the tin.

● Budget for enough paint for two

coats, especially over a previously painted surface.

● Try not to stop painting in the middle of a bare expanse of wall, because you may get a join mark where you stopped and started.

TO ESTIMATE WALL HEIGHT

If you need help estimating the height of walls, drop a weighted length of string from the top of a ladder or an upstairs window.

TO PAINT HIGH WALLS SAFELY

A scaffolding tower makes painting outside walls a lot easier. You can hire a tower from hire shops or large builders' merchants.

ENSURING A SOUND SURFACE

Before you begin:

● brush all surfaces to remove loose dirt, cobwebs and debris.

● Check for damage and strip off flaking paint.

● Fill cracks and repair any damaged rendering. Make sure window and door frames, other woodwork, guttering and pipework are in good condition before painting walls.

TO PAINT A PLANT-COVERED WALL

Prune any plants and then gently prise them off the wall. Protect them with a dust-sheet or large bin bags, securing the covering with masking tape or parcel tape. Use trellis when you replace the plants against the wall.

NEWLY RENDERED WALLS

New rendering (including pebbledash or spar dash and so on) needs a primer under paint.

Check with the company that applied the finish or the product manufacturer. Specialist or professional decorating suppliers offer a wider range of primers and products than many DIY stores and their staff are usually knowledgeable and helpful.

BRUSH OR ROLLER?

Use a large 100–150 mm (4 –6 in) brush, working the paint in well with the bristles, or an exterior, shaggy pile roller. Use a smaller brush for painting up to door and window frames.

GUTTERS AND DOWNPIPES

Some pipes and gutters may have been painted with bituminous paint and exterior gloss won't take directly over this stuff. To test for bituminous paint, put some petrol on a rag and rub it over the surface: if it picks up a reddish-brown colour the paint probably contains bitumen. Either use a bituminous paint again or apply aluminium primer-sealer, followed by an undercoat and then gloss.

TO PREPARE RUSTY PIPES

Rusted areas on metal pipework should be cleaned with wire wool or a wire brush and painted with a metal primer or rust inhibitor. If there is extensive damage you might consider replacing the pipes with plastic guttering.

TO PROTECT THE WALLS BEHIND PIPES

When you're painting downpipes, protect the wall behind by slotting in a length of card or hardboard to catch the splashes.

TO PAINT OR NOT TO PAINT PLASTIC?

It is not a good idea to paint plastic pipes as the paint flakes off easily after a while and they may look worse than before.

PAINTING WINDOWS AND DOORS

You should not have to strip off old paint unless it's in poor condition or paint build up over many years of redecorating is making it hard to close the windows or doors.

TO 'KEY' SOUND PAINTWORK

Sound paintwork can be keyed (to provide a suitable surface for the new paint to stick to) by washing it with sugar soap and water.

TO STRIP VARNISH

Washing soda solution and a scrubbing brush or wire scourer work well if you are planning on sanding the wood – it is cheaper than stripping varnished wood with a chemical stripper or varnish remover. Work on small sections and use a scraper to remove soggy varnish as you work.

TO SEAL KNOTS

On new wood, use a knotting compound on any knots to prevent the natural resin from bleeding through. Once this is done, it is best to go over surfaces by hand with fine abrasive paper and apply primer immediately.

TO PROTECT WOOD

Don't leave wood unprotected. If you've removed old paint, apply wood primer immediately. If the wood is treated with a preservative, apply a primer first. Follow this with an undercoat and exterior or interior gloss once it has dried.

EXTERIOR WINDOW FRAMES

Take particular care with windows (or windows in doors) to take about 2 mm of paint on to the glass to seal the edge of the wood. Otherwise a gap will allow rainwater to seep through.Use a small brush and work slowly and carefully.

TO PAINT BARGEBOARDS AND FASCIAS

You may have to remove gutters and downpipes in order to paint fascia boards. Knotting compound and primer are needed on bare wood. Check that surfaces are clean and apply undercoat: two coats may be necessary before you get a colour change. Sand down the surfaces with fine abrasive paper and apply gloss with a medium, 50–75 mm (2 –3 in) brush. Leave the first coat of gloss to dry for a minimum of 12 hours before applying a second coat.

WHEN TO PAINT THE OUTSIDE OF YOUR HOUSE

Spring or early autumn are the best times of year to do this. In summer, when it's hot, paint dries too quickly and you'll notice the smell more. When it's bitterly cold you don't want to be outside, perched on a ladder for hours on end. The best advice is to check the forecast and don't embark on painting if the weather is going to be changeable or damp.

WALLPAPERING

ESSENTIAL TOOLS

There are various tools that may be worthwhile if you do a lot of wallpapering, such as a seam roller to press edges, but a sponge or brush does the job as well. The following is a list of essentials.

● A lightweight folding wallpapering table, about 2 m (6½ ft) long and a bit wider than standard paper width.

● 12.5–15 cm (5–6 ins) paste brush and a bucket to mix the paste.

● Shears or fairly big scissors – the longer the better to make cutting a straight line easier.

● Small very sharp scissors to cut intricate nooks and crannies.

● A really sharp knife with replaceable blades. I like the type that you can snap off in sections.

● Walls are rarely straight, especially in older houses, so a plumb line is useful for checking the angles near corners. You can make one yourself out of string by tying a weight, such as a nut or bolt, on the end.

● A paper-hanging brush to smooth out paper and get rid of bubbles and creases. Be sure to keep this free of paste.

● A clean damp sponge to wipe any excess paste from the paper.

TO MAKE A BRUSH REST

Tie a length of string across the pasting bucket, from one handle to another, and you will have somewhere to rest your brush. You can wipe the brush across the string to control the amount of paste on it.

TO PAPER A CEILING

Try to construct a platform that runs the length of the room. Place this in the direction you will apply the paper. When standing on the platform, you should have about 7.5 cm (3 in) clearance between the top of your head and the ceiling.

TO MARK WALL FIXTURES

When you remove fixtures screwed into the wall, stick a matchstick in the hole, leaving about 5 mm (¼ inch) protruding. This will poke through the new paper as you press it on the wall, providing a marker for the replacement screw.

TO PAPER A NEW WALL

Brush with glue size to prevent the wall from absorbing water from the paste. You can mix up a weak solution of paste instead of size for this purpose.

TO PAPER AN OLD WALL

Make sure the surface is solid, not flaking, and fill any cracks. This is especially important if the wall has been damaged in the process of stripping it.

TO PAPER A DAMP WALL

If there's any sign of damage from damp, apply a coat of oil-based primer sealer to provide a good surface for the new paper.

TO WET PRE-PASTED PAPER

Remember to buy a trough to wet pre-pasted paper before hanging it. A perfectly clean plant trough can be used if you happen to have one the right size.

TO KEEP SCISSORS CLEAN

Dip them in a jar of hot water occasionally if they get paste on them, then wipe them dry. Scissors with paste on will be sticky and cutting paper with them is hopeless.

TO TRIM PAPER AT THE TOP OR BOTTOM

A metal L-shaped cutting guide can help to make sure you don't leave tiny gaps at the top or bottom of the wall.

TO MEASURE WALLS

Not many walls are a uniform height, so measure in several places around the room and use the longest as your standard for cutting lengths of wallpaper. Allow about 10 cm (2 in) extra for trimming.

TO MATCH A PATTERN

Cut the first length of paper and lay it flat. Then unroll the paper next to it and move it to match the pattern before cutting the next length. You could also just leave it a bit longer or shorter to help the match, and trim either more or less when it's on the wall – but it is not as economical as laying the paper down, especially for the first few lengths. You'll get a feel for the extra needed to match the pattern as you go.

TO CUT WALLPAPER

It is best to cut all the lengths needed before starting to paste. Number the lengths of paper in pencil on the back, according to how you are working around the room, so you know the order to hang them. Cut them long to allow for adjustments. Mark the top and bottom. Lay the pieces in order on the table, pattern-side down, ready to paste.

TO PASTE NEATLY

Brush the paste along the centre of the paper and work out to the edges. Fold the paper gently, pasted side to pasted side, in a concertina fashion as you work, so you can reach to the end of the length. Paste from left to right if you are right handed. Check that the paper is evenly covered, especially the edges.

TO AVOID BUBBLES IN PAPER

Once pasted, leave paper to soak according to the manufacturer's instructions. While thin paper or vinyl is ready almost immediately, heavier paper may need to stand for 10–15 minutes while you paste the rest. Otherwise bubbles will appear as the paper soaks up paste and expands on the wall. Usually, it contracts as it dries and the bubbles disappear, but not always!

TO AVOID SEEING SEAMS

Start hanging in the corner of a wall at right angles to the main window wall and work away from the window (the main source of light) so any slight overlaps in the paper won't cast shadows.

PREPARING THE FIRST LENGTH

Start in a corner and ensure a decent amount of paper turns the corner on to the wall with the window.. It's a good idea to use a plumb line to ensure that the paper hangs straight.

HANGING THE FIRST LENGTH

Start by pressing the paper on the wall, allowing about 5 cm (2 in) at the top for trimming. Work from the corner aligned with the straight pencil line. Allow the folds to drop out gently to avoid tearing the paper. Align the edge with the pencil line, taking care to keep the other side off of the wall. When it is aligned down one side, smooth the paper towards the opposite side and upwards using a paper-hanging brush or sponge, ensuring any bubbles are removed. Then work down from the centre to the outer edges, checking against the pencil mark as you go.

TRIMMING ALONG THE SKIRTING BOARD

If you don't have a trimming guide, run the back of a pair of scissors along the corner where the paper meets the skirting board to make a definite crease. Gently pull the paper away again and cut along this line before brushing the trimmed edge back into place.

TO STAY CLEAN AND TIDY

Put all the paper trimmings into a bin bag or other receptacle as you work – it's a good idea to hang or tape a bag on the back of the door (using masking tape). Wipe away any paste on the woodwork, paper or wall with a clean damp sponge.

TO NEATEN SEAMS

If you have a seam roller, run this lightly down the joins or use a clean sponge or brush. Be careful if the paper is textured as a roller may leave a mark on the surface.

TO TRIM PAPER WIDTH

In most houses the walls are not completely straight and the seams may slant alarmingly after negotiating a corner. The guiding principle is that if you need to mess with verticals and trim the edge of your paper at an angle, the best and most unobtrusive place to do this is in a corner.

TO PAPER A CHIMNEY BREAST

Start with a width of paper centred on the front of the chimney breast, then take it around the corners and on to the sides.

TO PAPER AROUND LIGHT SWITCHES

Always turn off electricity at the mains before you unscrew covers on switches. Allow about 1 cm (1/2 in) total extra paper to fit behind the switch cover. After loosening but before removing the switch cover, drop the pasted paper over it and cut an X in the middle of the area to be removed. Fold the paper from the centre back to the corners of the X and then trim off the paper from the middle, leaving about 5 mm (1/4 in) around the edge to fit under the switch cover. Once the paper is cut, remove the switch cover, tuck in the paper neatly and smooth the whole length of paper in place before replacing the switch cover.

If you cut too far, it's not a disaster as the paper usually sticks back neatly along a short cut.

TO PAPER AROUND FIREPLACES AND MANTELPIECES

This is a similar technique to papering around a door, but a little easier! Push the paper down on to the mantel and marking the outline of the mantel with the back of a pair of scissors. Then use the mark as a guide to cutting off excess. If paper becomes too dry while you are fiddling with the trimming, add fresh paste to the wall, rather than to the paper.

TO PAPER AN ARCHWAY

Leave about 2.5 cm (1 in) overlap into the arch and cut V-shapes into the overlap, from the wall to the edge of the paper. Paste the V-shapes into place on the arch, making sure the paper is flat on the wall and in the arch. Then cover the cuts in the paper with a strip carefully measured to fit the inside of the arch. It may be easier to use two strips, in which case they should meet with a join at the apex inside the arch.

TO PAPER A CEILING

Papering ceilings is a nightmare. Avoid it if you can. Textured paint is made specifically for improving poor ceiling surfaces or you could pay a plasterer to skim the ceiling (apply a thin layer of plaster) to give it a smooth finish for painting. If you have no choice other than to paper a ceiling, the following are a few tips. Continue until either the task is done or you're wrapped in sticky paper, weeping gently.
- Glue size will help prepare the surface to accept the paper.
- As a guide for applying the first length of paper, mark a straight line along the ceiling 1.5 cm (3/4 inch) less than the standard width of paper from the wall. You can buy chalk reels that dispense string coated with chalk to pin at one end and snap away from the ceiling to leave a straight line.
- Start hanging by the main light source (the window) and work parallel to and away from it so that overlapping seams don't cast shadows.
- Construct a safe platform on which to stand and walk as you press the paper in place, Make sure it is centred on the width of paper you are about to hang.
- Use a shrink-wrapped roll of paper to support the edge of the paper that will be applied to the ceiling first. Hold the folded concertina of pasted paper in the other hand. Unfold enough paper so you have plenty of slack to work with and simply (as they say) smooth the paper into the corner with your fingers. Remembering to follow the straight line and leaving the 1.5 cm (3/4 inch) overlap down the wall edge to be trimmed, unfold and apply the paper, smoothing it in place with a sponge or brush. The supporting roll of paper can also be used for this. When you're happy with it, go over the surface with a sponge, cloth or paper-hanging brush.
- Don't pull the paper in your hand or it will take the paper you've just hung off the ceiling. Be sure you have plenty of slack and keep your supporting hand close. Trim around the ceiling rose, following instructions for immovable fixtures above.

TO MAKE CEILING PAPER STICK

If the paper pulls easily away from the ceiling as you are working, the most likely cause is that the paste is too weak. Make up a fresh batch with less water and start again. If you need to add more paste to already pasted sections, always add it to the ceiling and not to the paper.

PICTURES AND MIRRORS

You may be lucky enough to have picture rails for hanging picture and mirrors, but most houses don't have them.

THE IDEAL HOOK

If your plaster is fairly sound then a simple pin hook will support a light picture. You can buy them with two pins for heavier weight pictures, or you can spread the load by using two hooks near to the edges of the picture.

A hard plaster wall will not take normal picture hooks, but you can buy plastic hooks specially made for hard plaster. These have three or four little pins, which makes them easier to hammer in.

HOW TO HANG A PICTURE

Decide where you want the top of the picture to rest against the wall and mark it lightly with a pencil. The hook needs to be placed below the pencil mark.Check this before you start by holding the picture against the wall.

The cord should be about two thirds of the way up the picture back and should be roughly the same width as the frame but under no tension.

A common mistake when hanging pictures is to place them too high. Ideally, a picture should be hung at eye level.

FINDING THE RIGHT PLACE

Spend some time experimenting, to work out where you want your pictures to hang. Prop them against a wall or get someone to hold them in place. Then take time to decide exactly where you want to hang them.

GROUPING PICTURES

One large picture or photograph can make a statement on a blank wall, but groups can look good too. Try making a theme, maybe flowers, animals, churches, or even similar colours.

HANGING A MIRROR

Mirrors can be heavy and need a strong picture hook and proper cord on which to hang. Never use parcel string or garden twine, particularly for a heavy mirror.

Mirrors are good for making a narrow hallway seem wider and for bringing light into a room. Place the mirror near or opposite a window for good results.

INDOOR GARDENING
& PETS

This chapter covers gardening in the home, with tips and ideas on the care of houseplants, planting bulbs for Christmas and flower arranging. You will find ideas on how to prolong the life of plants, given as presents, which will bloom for years in the garden, reminding you of the giver. And there is helpful advice on choosing and caring for pets as well as keeping chickens – the latest in 'Urban Chick' – so that you can experience the joy of collecting your own eggs.

Whether you have a conservatory, greenhouse, balcony or window box, you can grow your own plants and flowers to fill the house with colour and fresh scents.

HOUSEPLANTS

TO REMOVE APHIDS
This works for green and white fly, and other nasty little things that invade and make a sticky mess. Sprinkle a few spoonfuls of cold, soapy washing-up water over the infested parts of the plants. Repeat as necessary.

WATER FOR HOUSEPLANTS
Save the water from boiling eggs to water your plants as it is full of minerals. Water from an aquarium or goldfish bowl is also excellent for houseplants.

TO WATER EASILY
A clean, well-rinsed washing-up liquid bottle makes an ideal indoor watering can, enabling you to control the water and avoid spilling it on your furniture.

DON'T DROWN PLANTS
Roots need air as well as water. Keeping the compost soaked all the time means death for most plants, so take care not to over-water potted plants. It is usually best to put water into the container, rather than directly on to the topsoil.

WATERING WHEN YOU'RE ON HOLIDAY
Lay an old towel in the bottom of the bath and stand your potted plants on it, without the saucers. Fill the bath with 8-10 cm (3-4 in) of water. So long as all your pots have holes in the bottom, the plants will automatically be watered.

TO MAKE LEAVES SHINE
Gently wipe a little glycerine (from the chemist or with the baking ingredients in shops) over houseplant leaves. Alternatively, mix a little milk with an equal amount of water and use this to wipe the leaves. The inside of a banana skin can also be used to wipe plant leaves.

TOO DRAUGHTY
Plants don't like draughts, so try not to place them in the following positions:
- between closed curtains and a window
- near an air-conditioning duct
- on a windowsill with a poor fitting frame
- near or above a radiator

ALL-IMPORTANT LIGHT
Plants need daylight in order to grow healthy; they will not thrive in an unlit corner or dark passageway.

PLANT HYGIENE
It is really important to keep plants healthy. Remove any fallen or discoloured leaves and snip off flower heads as soon as they die. Debris in the pot encourages mould.

TO DETER CATS FROM DIGGING IN PLANT POTS
Dip cotton wool balls into oil of cloves (available from the chemist) and put these just under the soil line in your plant pots. Cats do not like the smell of cloves.

POT BOUND?

This is how to recognise when a plant is pot bound.

- When the roots appear through the drainage hole.
- The soil dries out very quickly between waterings.
- The stem and leaf growth seem very slow.
- The final check: gently turn the pot upside down, supporting the plant on your hand, and ease out of the pot with a twist. If it is pot bound the roots will look matted and not much soil will be visible.

RE-POTTING

Spring is the best time. Select a new pot, which is only slightly larger than the existing one, and quarter fill it with compost. Water the compost well. Remove the plant from the existing pot and place it on top of the compost. Gradually fill in around it with compost, firming it down as you go. The plant stem should be at the same level as before. Tap the pot to settle the compost. Water carefully and place in the shade for a week.

SOOTHING ALOE VERA

Break the leaves or spikes off an aloe vera plant and the sticky liquid that pours out can be rubbed straight on your hands to soften the skin or used to ease a minor burn or sunburnt skin.

TO PROPAGATE ALOE VERA

These plants make good gifts and are easy to propagate as they take root easily. Pull off a spike or leaf, lay it against the side of a pot and fill the pot with compost.

GROWING CITRUS PIPS

This is good fun! You may not harvest your own oranges or lemons, but the stylish plants have shiny green leaves – for free. Plant two or three pips to a small pot in potting compost, just covering them. Water well and put in a warm place. Cover with a piece of glass or tie a polythene bag around the pot until the seedlings appear. Make sure that the glass or polythene doesn't touch the seedlings. If all of the pips sprout, transplant the strongest into separate pots.

PREPARED BULBS

Prepared bulbs are commercially stored in temperature-controlled conditions to encourage early growth and flowering .

CHOOSING HYACINTHS FOR CHRISTMAS FLOWERING

The bulbs must be the prepared type (see above). Choose the same named bulb for each bowl as different types come up unevenly if mixed together. Blue hyacinths have by far the best perfume (and these are usually the first to sell out in the shops). Bulbs are available from late August or early September onwards.

TO PLANT HYACINTHS FOR CHRISTMAS

Plant in September or October. If you use a container without drainage holes, put a few stones in the bottom. Fill about half full with potting compost, press down and pop the bulbs on top. You can plant them quite close together. Fill to the top with compost, pressing down well between the bulbs so that the tops are level with the surface of the soil . Water well – it takes time for the water to seep into the compost.

Put the bowl loosely into a plastic carrier bag in a warm dark place, such as the bottom of a wardrobe or under the stairs. Check to make sure the soil stays damp and bring into a room when the bulbs shoots are about 2.5 cm (1 inch) high. They will be very pale, but soon turn green. Keep the compost well watered. If, as often happens, the flowers are heavy headed and keep falling over, cut them and place in water where they will last just as long. Next time you're in the florist, make a note of how much cut hyacinths cost! When the bulbs have finished flowering, plant them in the garden (see page 158), where they'll continue to bloom.

PLANTING BULBS TO FLOWER IN THE HOUSE AT CHRISTMAS

Crocuses and other small bulbs cannot be bought prepared for early flowering, so have to be treated in a different way to hyacinths. In September/October choose a container with drainage holes or place some 'crocks' (bits of broken plant pot or some stones) in the bottom. Three-quarters fill the pot with compost, place the bulbs on top, quite closely together, and add more compost to cover the tips of the bulbs completely. Firm down the surface and place the pot in the garden. When the bulbs have grown and the flower buds are just showing, bring the pot into the house to encourage the bulbs to flower. After flowering, the bulbs can be left to die down and then planted in the garden, where they will continue to bloom for years.

FLOWERING HOUSE PLANTS

CHRYSANTHEMUMS

They are probably the most popular flowering house plants, and each year thousands are thrown away when they could be planted in the garden. If they survive, chrysanthemums continue to flower outdoors for years. After the plants have finished flowering, leave them in a cool, but frost-free, area to die down naturally. Water sparingly and plant outdoors between April and September. They will continue to give pleasure and provide colour in your garden .

CYCLAMEN

These are available from September until Christmas. When they have finished flowering, which could be as long as two months, reduce the watering and place the pot in a cool, light and frost-free area. The leaves will wither and you may think the plant is dead. Don't worry; start watering it again in August and the tuber will slowly come back to life. It will resprout and flower buds will appear. Bring the plant into the house and start feeding it weekly. Always water cyclamen from below; never let water stand on the fleshy tuber.

AZALEAS

They like to be kept wet while flowering. The best method of watering is immersion: stand the whole pot in water to just below the rim and leave to soak until the compost surface glistens and looks wet. Then lift out and allow the plant to drain. Once the plant has finished flowering transfer it to a cool, frost-free place and continue to water. When there is no danger of frost, put the pot in a shady area of the garden. Keep watering and feeding it. Bring back into the house in September when flowering buds have appeared.

POLYANTHUS (PRIMULA)

These small, brightly coloured pot plants, which look like primroses, can be transplanted into the garden when they have finished flowering indoors. Give them time to die down in a cool, frost-free area before planting out. You may think they look sad, but next spring, and in the following years, they should revive and continue to flower.

FLOWER ARRANGING

TO KEEP TULIPS UPRIGHT

Make a hole by sticking a pin completely through the top of the stem just below the flower head. This really does work!

WILD FLOWERS

They look good in vases or jars, especially with grasses and herbs such as mint, rosemary and lavender. Reserve a corner of your garden for wild flowers (you can buy the seeds).

Selecting the occasional head of a prolific hedgerow 'weed' may be acceptable, but picking flowers from the wild is not a good idea – some wild flowers are endangered and/or protected and should not be picked at all.

TO MAKE WOODY STEMMED FLOWERS LAST LONGER

Roses and other woody stemmed flowers last longer in water when any leaves that might be in the water are trimmed off. Then use a rolling pin or hammer to bash the ends of the stems – this allows them to take up water more easily.

ARRANGING TIP

Arrange large flowers first, and get the balance right, before popping in smaller flowers and greenery to fill the gaps.

103

TO KEEP FLOWERS UPRIGHT IN AN ARRANGEMENT

Plastic hair rollers are really good: stand them upright in the bottom of the vase. Support the flower stems in the rollers. Don't use a see-through container though!

LONGER LASTING FLOWERS

If you don't have one of those sachets from the florist, a teaspoon of sugar works well. Alternatively, dissolve two aspirin tablets in warm water and add them to the vase water.

TO REVIVE WILTING FLOWERS

Try snipping off about 2.5 cm (1 inch) from the ends of the stalks, remove any dead leaves and then return the flowers to a washed vase of cold water.

FLOWERS THAT ARE TOO SHORT

If the stems are too short for your vase, support them in plastic drinking straws and cut these to length to suit the vase.

TWICE AS GOOD

Stand your flower arrangement in front of a mirror. It will seem as though it contains twice as many flowers as well as making twice the impact.

TO CLEAN FLOWER VASES

This is especially good for glass. Fill the vase with warm water, and add one or two denture cleaning tablets (depending on the size of vase). Leave to soak overnight. Rinse thoroughly and wash in the normal way.

TO CLEAN ARTIFICIAL FLOWERS

Whether they are silk or polyester, single or an arrangement, place them in a large polythene carrier bag (check that there are no holes) with at least 4 tablespoons of table salt. Close the bag and shake gently for a few minutes. Then shake each individual flower to remove the salt. The salt may look clean, but if you run water into it you'll see how much dirt has been removed.

PETS

NEUTRALIZE PET-URINE ODOUR

This applies particularly to carpets. Make up a solution of a quarter white vinegar to three-quarters water. Test a small area of fabric in an inconspicuous place first, before treating a large area.

TO HELP ELIMINATE SMELLS FROM CAT LITTER TRAYS

Put a thin layer of bicarbonate of soda in the bottom of the tray, then sprinkle in the litter as normal. The cat won't notice!

PET ACCIDENT ON THE CARPET?

Clean up as best you can in the normal way. Mix lemon juice into cream of tartar (available with other baking ingredients) to make a thin paste. Apply this to the marked carpet and leave to dry. Vacuum and rinse the area with warm water to finish.

TO REMOVE PET HAIR FROM UPHOLSTERY

Try these suggestions.
- Dampen a sponge and wipe over the furniture, rinsing the sponge as necessary.
- Put on rubber gloves and dampen them slightly. Wipe your hands in a downward motion over the furniture.
- Wrap wide sticky tape around your hand, sticky side out, and swipe or pat it over the furniture. Change the tape when it is covered with hairs.

TO TRAIN YOUR KITTEN

To train your kitten not to play with (attack) house plants, use a clean plant spray and clean water. Lay in wait, then gently spray a little moisture over the kitten as it attacks the plant. Cats hate the damp and being caught once or twice will do the trick. This is a good way of training kittens not to get up to other unacceptable tricks – such as leaping on to a kitchen work surface.

PET PATIENCE

Remember that animals do not set out to irritate or anger you — they simply behave like animals! If they do something that seems 'wrong', they do it because it is 'right' to them. So, have a little patience while you train them.

DOGS

BUYING AN ADULT DOG

Try to find out some of the dog's history as it is important to check that it will fit into your lifestyle.

BUYING A PUPPY

Puppies should generally leave their mothers at 8 weeks old.

VACCINATIONS

Puppies should be vaccinated against distemper and hard-pad at 8 weeks old, before they mix with other dogs. They need regular boosters, particularly if you want to put them in kennels.

COLLARS

The British law says that all dogs, when out in public, must wear a collar with the owner's name and telephone number on it.

BONES

Never give a bone to a puppy under one year old. Dogs like chewing on things and to stop it ruining your best shoes, buy marrow bones or dog chews.

ESSENTIAL WATER

Always leave out a bowl filled with water for dogs of all ages.

FEEDING

The following guidelines will keep your dog healthy and happy.
- Puppy: 3–4 meals a day of recommended puppy food
- 6 months: 3 meals a day as above
- 6–12 months: 2 meals a day, a mixture of half canned meat and half dry mix
- Adult: 1 meal a day, as above

TRAINING

It is vital for all dogs to be trained and it should start when they are puppies – with toilet training, learning their names, and getting used to a collar and lead. Be patient, keep commands simple, give praise when they obey and a firm 'no' if they don't.

EXERCISE

Dogs need exercise. The extent depends on the breed, but two daily walks off the lead should be the minimum.

BATHS

Dogs also need baths. You will know when. Use warm water and a dog shampoo. Rinse and dry well, using an old towel kept especially for the purpose.

DO NOT TEASE A DOG

It will become very confused and unpredictable.

DON'T LEAVE A DOG IN A HOT CAR

Never leave dogs in cars in hot weather as they will become overheated and distressed.

TO STOP DOGS STEALING FOOD

Try to think in terms of the dog that steals food needs an owner who puts food away. The point is that dogs do not know that they are stealing – they think the food is left out for them.

CATS

They make wonderful pets and can be great companions. They are independent and can almost manage on their own, although they can get lonely. A cat will love and cherish you if you look after it well. It is acknowledged that stroking a cat can be very calming and can help you to relax at the end of a hard day. Adult cats are especially good pets for people who don't want a very demanding or active companion.

BUYING A KITTEN

Kittens should be at least 7–8 weeks old before leaving their mothers. Their eyes should be bright, coats shiny and healthy looking, and they should have clean ears and a dry tail.

TOILET TRAINING

Kittens are easy to train with a litter tray and proprietary litter. (A mother cat will begin training her kittens.) A cat flap is a good idea once the cat is allowed out and familiar with its surroundings. When your kitten is used to the tray, put the tray outdoors and the kitten will gradually learn to use the flap and then the garden.

VACCINATIONS

At 12 weeks kittens should be vaccinated against enteritis and cat flu. They need regular boosters, especially if you want to put them into a cattery. They may need worming, which you can do yourself, and the pet shop or vet can advise on products.

NEUTERING

Cats can, and will, start breeding at 5 months (occasionally earlier). It is advisable and responsible to have both males and females neutered. Your vet will advise on when and how. It does cost a little more for females because it is a more complicated procedure.

FEEDING

Cats need a good balanced diet. There are excellent canned foods and you will soon discover which is your cat's favourite (usually the most expensive). You can use a dried food but you must always make sure you leave out plenty of water for the cat to drink. Kittens drink milk but cats prefer water; kittens and cats may be allergic to milk and it may give them diarrhoea. Adult cats will occasionally chew grass, which is good for their digestion.

FLEAS

Cats do get fleas. Look out for excessive scratching and tiny brown flecks in their fur (particularly next to their skin); you will probably get bitten as well. You can put a flea collar on the cat or ask the vet for advice as there are many excellent products for getting rid of the fleas and keeping them at bay in the future.

CATCHING MICE AND BIRDS

Cats are bred to catch these. They will bring mice into the house and present them to you (usually dead) and you will be expected to praise them for their exploits.

Birds are a different matter: the statistics for the numbers of birds that cats kill are horrific. If you want to feed the birds make sure you have a high bird table and that your cat wears a collar with a bell attached. The cat may not like the bell at first but it will warn the birds that a cat is near.

TOYS FOR KITTENS AND CATS

There are dozens of 'toys' in pet shops and anything with catnip in it will be popular. Even a cotton reel on a piece of string will provide hours of pleasure. Make sure the kitten does not become entangled with string and choke – a ball of wool is not a good plaything for a kitten.

GOLDFISH

You may start with one or two fish from the fairground but if looked after carefully, they will live for years (and grow in size too). Although they are 'only fish' they can give great pleasure. I have looked after goldfish for friends and always feel they recognise me when I visit. They get to know who feeds them and will quiver against the sides of the tank.

TO CLEAN A FISH TANK

Every 2-3 months is recommended with a filter, every 2-3 weeks without. Put the fish in a bowl with tap water at room temperature. The old tank water is good on the garden. Scrub the tank well with clean water only. Refill the tank with cold tap water and add a proprietary product to regulate the additives in the tap water. Follow the instructions closely and let the water come back to room temperature before putting the fish back in.

WATER SNAILS

These will live happily with the fish and eat all the algae that makes the tank green and slimy. Remember to put them in the bowl with the fish while you clean the tank. You can buy water snails at the pet shop. A friend of mine took some out of a neighbour's garden pond and they have been living with his fish (and doing a good cleaning job) for two years.

FEEDING

Feed fish twice a day (check for other varieties of goldfish) with a good proprietary dried fish food. Buy some 'water weeds' and a few objects for them to swim through.

FILTER PUMP

A pump helps to aerate the tank water. This is not absolutely necessary but it will help to keep the tank clean and the fish seem to enjoy the bubbles.

TROPICAL FISH

Tropical fish are different from ordinary goldfish. They need specially controlled conditions, with heat, light, a filter and careful feeding. Find out about how to keep them from a good shop before buying any on a whim.

BUDGERIGARS

Members of the parrot family, budgerigars (also known as parakeets) are native to Australia. They are the most popular caged birds and come in a huge range of colours and varieties. They are easy to keep, and love to be held, stroked and to interact with humans. You can also teach them to talk. They can live to be 20 years old, although 8 years is more likely in captivity.

CAGE

Buy a good large cage from a pet shop and hang it somewhere high, out of draughts. Budgies like toys, bells, a ladder, plenty of room to perch and a mirror in which to preen themselves. Clean the cage out at least once a week. Make sure you close windows and doors when you let your budgie out of the cage to clean it or for exercise flights. Otherwise they will be out and away, and wild birds do not treat them kindly.

FEEDING

Give budgies mixed seed, bought at the pet shop, a cuttlefish bone to sharpen and trim their beaks, and plenty of water to drink. They like to take baths too. Budgies also eat fruit and vegetables, but not cabbage or lettuce.

HAMSTERS & GUINEA PIGS

All hamsters are descended from three golden hamsters (one male and two females), found by a zoologist in Syria in 1930. They are lively animals and like to be handled. Start off with a little cherishing and gradually build up the handling; don't squeeze them hard though or they will bite.

Guinea pigs are often known as 'cavys'. They are native to South America where they live in the wild. Guinea pigs usually live from 5-7 years in captivity.

Both hamsters and guinea pigs make great pets for children.

for pets) and plenty of hay. Hamsters need sawdust to burrow in; hay and wood shavings (bought from the pet shop) are good. Avoid any from building timber treated with preservatives that may be harmful to pets. Hamsters also like bits of (safe) wood to gnaw and items to climb over and into – a cardboard toilet-roll middle or a cardboard box with a hole cut in it are good hiding places, and a wheel (not metal) to tread round. Guinea pigs should have a 'run' so that they can move around on grass outside the cage.

BUYING AS A PET

Buy a hamster at 4–8 weeks old. It should look lively, with bright eyes and a healthy coat. Syrian or golden hamsters should always be kept alone in one cage – if they are put together they will fight and may kill each other. Dwarf hamsters (Russian or Chinese) can be kept in pairs, but it is not advisable.

Two guinea pigs are better than one as they like a companion. Two females are best; a pair of males must have been together from a very young age.

CAGES AND RUNS

This should be large and strong, with a solid bottom and a ventilated top. Line it with newspaper and then lay down sawdust or wood shavings (suitable

FEEDING

You can buy specialist food from the pet shop and top it up with green vegetable leaves, beetroot, celery and fruit. Never give any meats. Make sure there is always plenty of drinking water. Hamsters eat almost anything vegetarian and love apples and pears. Guinea pigs like carrots and broccoli. Be sure to wash bought produce thoroughly to remove all traces of harmful pesticides, but don't give anything too wet as this will upset the animals' stomachs. For a treat, try raisins, currants and shelled nuts.

CLEANING THE CAGE

The cage needs cleaning out at least once a week. Be sure to remove all uneaten fruit and vegetables before they go mouldy.

Keeping Chickens

KEEPING CHICKENS is a marvellous hobby and collecting fresh eggs that your chickens have laid is one of life's great pleasures.

You need to know what you are doing and prepare suitable housing for your chickens. We all know about cunning foxes and their reputation is justified. They are very clever at getting into chicken runs and, once inside, they cause carnage. If this happens it is heartbreaking, so get the right living quarters and make sure you shut the chickens in every night.

Children will be delighted to help with this task. An excellent website with loads of information on keeping chickens is: www.omlet.co.uk

EGGS
Some hens will lay up to eight eggs a week at times. They start at 20 weeks old and after a year of laying they usually go into a moulting period. Don't panic – this is when their plumage is rejuvenated. This phase usually lasts for 4–6 weeks, during which time they will lay fewer eggs. Chickens are known as 'off lay' during this period.

BROODY HENS
Hens often decide to sit on an egg to hatch it into a chick (even without any cockerels about). They will fluff themselves up and sit all day, and continue for up to three weeks (the incubating period for eggs). It is best to take the egg away, being careful not to get pecked (it's a good idea to wear thick gloves). You can buy pottery eggs to replace the stolen egg, if you don't want the chicken to get too upset!

◀ **CHICKENS MAKE GOOD PETS** for children, who love to look after them and collect the eggs. Here, the author and her brother watch spellbound as their hens peck at the grain they've put out for them.

NESTING BOXES

Whether individual or open, these need to be regularly filled with clean hay and straw. You should collect eggs at least once a day. This helps to prevent hens from becoming broody and means you can keep a good eye on the hens and the hen house (to make sure the fox stays away).

FEEDING

Chickens need a proprietary feed once a day and you can give them scraps as well. They are not greedy animals and eat only as much as they need, so you will not over-feed them. They like pasta, fruit, vegetables (broccoli, Brussels sprouts and spinach are good for yellow yolks) and, occasionally, cake. For a real – but rare – treat try Marmite on bread! Never feed them meat or anything too salty (so Marmite treats must be small and few and far between). If they don't like it they won't eat it. Make sure that there is always lots of water available and there should be plenty of 'grit' to peck at, as this helps the egg shells to form.

HEALTHY HENS

When they are fully grown hens should look healthy and perky. They should have bright red combs when they are 'in lay' and when you pick them up their bodies should feel plump and firm.

CHICKEN MANURE

This is great for the garden but it must be kept for at least a year before spreading, otherwise it will burn the plants. Store it in an outhouse or log store until you are ready to use it.

A CUSTOM-BUILT HOUSE FOR YOUR HENS

If you're good at carpentry – or know someone who is – you could build a raised hen house in a secluded part of the garden. There are also companies that sell them, so check magazines or the Internet for details if you're after something specially designed for hens.

HEALTH &
BEAUTY

There is a wealth of tips and ideas on health and beauty, some as old as our grandparents (but none the less good for that) and others more modern. I've selected the ones I find most useful, and hope you will try them.

Try to avoid using cosmetic products that contain hazardous man-made chemicals, especially for babies and children; you'll find plenty on the market that are free from these harmful ingredients.

Feeling good and looking good go hand in hand. Natural therapies and remedies can help you to relax and kick off the stresses and strains of life.

WELLBEING

ESSENTIAL OILS FOR YOUR BATH

Lavender and camomile will relax you, relieve stress and help you to sleep. Use 6–8 drops of oil in your bath. Do not use if you have very sensitive skin. Rosemary oil (also 6-8 drops) is good for aching muscles and stiff joints – perfect after a work out at the gym or a day's toil in the garden. Always check the suitability of oils if you are pregnant.

FOR A FRAGRANT, SPICY BATH

Try grating allspice berries straight into your bath – they're mildly antiseptic and aromatic.

A GINGER BATH

For a really refreshing bath-time treat, grate a piece of fresh root ginger into a small muslin or cotton bag. Dangle this under the running tap as you fill your bath. This stimulates and invigorates the circulation.

A VERY RELAXING DRINK

Camomile tea has a subtle, warming flavour; a cup at bedtime can really help you to sleep.

TO ASSIST SLEEP

Sprinkle a little lavender oil on your pillow. It helps you to relax, smells lovely and is very soothing.

TO KEEP COOL ON A HOT NIGHT

Cotton or linen sheets do help and so does sprinkling baby powder on them, as it helps to absorb moisture. If you don't have baby powder, try a little cornflour.

RUN OUT OF DEODORANT?

Try rubbing on a slice of lemon instead – this can be a powerful and effective alternative to commercial products.

ESSENTIAL OILS TO RELIEVE A BLOCKED CHEST AND SINUSES

Use either peppermint or eucalyptus oil. Add 3–5 drops of oil to a bowl of hot water. Cover your head with a towel, lean over the steam from the bowl and breathe in deeply. You'll soon feel your airways beginning to clear. Do not use if you're asthmatic.

TO SOOTHE ACHING JOINTS

Mix together 1 tablespoon of olive oil, 4 drops of eucalyptus oil and 3 drops of lavender oil. Massage this into stiff and aching joints.

TO EASE AN IMPENDING MIGRAINE

If you feel a migraine coming on, it is worth applying a warm compress of marjoram to the back of your neck. This helps to dilate blood vessels in your neck area.

TO HELP RELIEVE A HEADACHE

Lavender oil again (the Victorians and Edwardians swore by it and would put lavender water on their linen to make it smell beautiful and to deter insects). It is too strong to be used neat on your skin, so dilute it with a carrier oil, such as sweet almond or grape-seed. Massage gently on your temple and forehead in a circular motion using just your fingertips.

TO HELP RELIEVE THE SYMPTOMS OF A HEAD COLD

Try soaking your feet in a bowl of hot water with 2 teaspoons of English mustard powder added. This draws the blood to the feet and helps to relieve congestion.

A SIMPLE GARGLE FOR A SORE THROAT

Try adding a tablespoon of vinegar (cider vinegar is best) to a glass of warm water. You can also gargle with half a teaspoon of salt in a glass of warm water – particularly if you are losing your voice.

HOME-MADE COUGH MIXTURE

Mix 4 tablespoons of honey with 2 tablespoons of glycerine and the juice of 2 lemons. Take as you wish. It is very soothing at night to help you sleep.

TO OVERCOME NAUSEA

• Peppermint oil helps to stop you feeling sick. Try sprinkling a little on a tissue or handkerchief and then inhale deeply.

• Recent research has shown that ginger is excellent for settling the stomach. It can be used as a remedy for travel sickness. Try sipping ginger ale, chewing on ginger biscuits or drinking the ginger drink that follows. At least 20 minutes before a car or ferry journey, try taking $1/4$ teaspoon of powdered ginger in a little water or chew some fresh root ginger.

TO MAKE A GINGER DRINK

Chop a large knob of ginger, about 50 g (2 oz), into small pieces (there's no need to peel it). Place in a saucepan with 900 ml ($1^{1}/_{2}$ pints) water and bring to the boil. Turn down the heat to very low and cover the pan. Simmer for 20 minutes. Add 2 teaspoons of honey and stir until melted. When it's cool, add the juice of 1 lemon, cover and put in the fridge. Strain before drinking. This is very good when you've been sick and don't feel like eating anything. It is also refreshing on a hot day.

WHEN YOU HAVE UNCOMFORTABLE COLD SORES

You'll find it much easier to sip your drink through a straw – a flexible one is best.

TO HELP RELIEVE INDIGESTION

Peppermint tea aids digestion after a rich meal. It's also very cooling served iced in summer.

A HELPFUL DIURETIC

Nettle tea has a pleasant flavour. It can work as a diuretic and also aids digestion.

TO KEEP YOUR BREATH SWEET

Chewing fresh parsley or fennel or caraway seeds freshens the breath and is particularly effective (and useful) after eating a garlic-rich or spicy meal.

TO DETER FLIES AND MOSQUITOES

Moisten some cotton wool with a little water, put it on a small dish or saucer and sprinkle with a few drops of citronella oil. Replenish the cotton wool every few days. This is very effective in the bedroom, particularly at night when a buzzing mosquito can irritate and cause havoc.

TO TREAT MOSQUITO AND OTHER INSECT BITES

Apply a compress of warm salty water to relieve the itching.
A good dab of vinegar also works.
Try applying a paste, made of bicarbonate of soda and water, to the sting.

TO REMOVE A PLASTER WITHOUT THE OUCH!

Rub baby oil into the plaster and surrounding area. This should help to ease the pain when ripping off the plaster. This is a particularly good tip for children, who tend to anticipate the pain!

HAIR CARE

SHORT OF SHAMPOO?

Good-quality natural soap (bars or liquid) work just as well.

SOLID SHAMPOO

Some beauty shops sell both solid shampoo and conditioner bars, which are particularly good for travelling. Drain well after use.

TO USE CONDITIONER

Smother conditioner on the ends of the hair, but don't take it to the roots. Natural oils keep the roots well conditioned. Regular conditioner needs to be left in the hair for 30 seconds, no longer.

MAKE YOUR SHAMPOO AND CONDITIONER GO FURTHER

When the bottle is nearly empty, remove the lid and pour in 2–3 tablespoons of warm water. Put the lid back on, give a good shake and it will last for at least a couple more washes.

TO MAKE A HAIR CONDITIONER

● Pour 300 ml (½ pint) boiling water over 3–4 short fresh rosemary stems and leave to steep for an hour. Strain and use the water as a final rinse. This leaves most types of hair beautifully soft and fragrant.
● Try this to make your hair shine. Lightly beat 1 egg and a little milk. Run this mixture through your hair and leave for 5 minutes. Then rinse off with cool water, and dry as normal.

TRY THIS ANCIENT INCA RECIPE TO NOURISH YOUR HAIR

Mash ½ avocado, 1 tablespoon of olive oil, ½ small banana and 1 egg yolk. Gently massage this cream into your hair and scalp. Cover with a shower cap, and leave for 1 hour. Rinse well with warm water and shampoo as usual.

DULL HAIR?

The main cause of dull hair (if you are fit and well, and eating a good diet) is too much 'product' and not enough rinsing. Rinse for 2–3 minutes until your hair feels really clean and then rinse again for another 10 seconds!
● A good rinse with cider vinegar and warm water – about 1 tablespoon of cider vinegar to 600 ml (1 pint) water – every couple of weeks also helps to stop 'product' build up.

● Instead of buying an expensive cleansing shampoo to remove a bad build up of conditioner, wax or gel, about once a year wash with a little good-quality 'eco' washing-up liquid. Rinse thoroughly and use a light conditioner on the ends – your hair will be satin-soft and glossy.

TO GIVE HAIR A SHINE

Try to use cold water for the last rinse. This flattens the hair cuticles and makes hair shinier.

TO AVOID DAMAGING WET HAIR

Hair is fragile when wet, so use only a wide-toothed comb, not a brush, which can damage the hair.

TO GIVE FINE HAIR VOLUME

Blow dry your hair with you head down, concentrating on the roots. This also helps keep hair straight.

TO TREAT GREASY HAIR

A good dash of cider vinegar in the water for the last rinse counteracts alkaline shampoo and helps to keep hair shiny and manageable.

TO CALM CURLS AND FRIZZ

Avoid towel drying your hair as this makes it frizzy. When dry, finish with a small blob of smoothing hair serum.

NO TIME TO WASH YOUR HAIR?

Shake a little talcum powder on to your crown and give it a good brush through. The fairer you are the better this works. Brush dark hair more thoroughly to avoid looking grey!

HOMEMADE HAIR MASK

1 ripe banana
2 teaspoons grapeseed oil (from health food shops)
cling film

This mask is perfect for dry and damaged hair. Peel and mash the banana, then mix in the oil to make a thick paste. Massage this into dry hair and the scalp. Wrap your hair in cling film and leave for 30 minutes. Wash out the mask with a mild shampoo.

TO PREVENT STATIC BUILD UP

Try using a metal comb.

TO CLEAN BRUSHES AND COMBS

Dirty brushes and combs can deposit old styling products and grease on your hair. Remove trapped hair and then wash the brush or comb carefully in warm water with a little washing-up liquid or shampoo. Rinse thoroughly and dry well.
● For a deeper clean, after removing trapped hair, wash in warm water with a few washing soda crystals added, rinse thoroughly and dry well.

COFFEE HAIR COLOUR FOR BRUNETTES AND REDHEADS

After washing your hair in the normal way, use a final rinse of warm, freshly ground coffee (not instant) - three cupfuls should be enough. Don't rinse this out. It will make your hair a rich colour with a shine to it.

FACE

SHORT OF SUNSCREEN FOR YOUR NOSE?

... and other extremities when sun-bathing nude. Zinc and castor oil cream, the sort used on babies' bottoms, works really well.

TO REMOVE GLITTER AND HEAVY MAKE-UP

Gently rub in a tiny amount of Vaseline, taking care not to get any glitter in your eyes. Wash your face well with warm soapy water.

TO WHITEN TEETH

Dip a damp toothbrush in bicarbonate of soda and brush your teeth. It is slightly abrasive and will polish teeth without damaging the enamel.

TO REMOVE THE SMELL OF GARLIC FROM YOUR BREATH

Try chewing any of these: fresh parsley, mint or celery, fennel or cardamom seeds, or a coffee bean.

SWOLLEN EYES (NON-MEDICAL)

Place thin slices of cucumber over each eyelid, renewing them as soon as they are warm. If you don't have cucumber, use cold damp teabags or witch hazel on cotton wool pads. Lie down and relax for 30 minutes whilst you are doing this.

DARK CIRCLES UNDER THE EYES?

Peel and grate a potato (not a new potato) and wrap it in a piece of muslin or a clean disposable kitchen cloth. Apply this directly to the area beneath your eye and leave it on for about 20 minutes. Don't allow the potato juice to come in contact with your eye. Wipe away the starchy residue, rinse, and you'll find that the dark circles will be greatly reduced.

TO SOFTEN GOOEY MASCARA

Try blotting the wand on kitchen paper. Toilet paper is too soft and will leave fibres on the brush.

TO CONDITION DRY LASHES

Before you go to bed, remove your eye make-up in the normal way, then dab a tiny bit of Vaseline on your lashes. Remove it in the morning before applying mascara.

MAKE THE MOST OF MASCARA

Always begin with thoroughly clean lashes; coating over yesterday's mascara will lead to brittle lashes. Try using a lash comb to comb your lashes gently after applying mascara. It separates them and removes any unwanted blobs. Two light coats of mascara is better than one heavy coat; allow the first to dry before applying the second.

TO GIVE YOUR FACE A SAUNA

This is especially good for stressed skin and a good method of cleansing body toxins. Fill a bowl with almost-boiling water and add four drops of essential oil to suit your skin type:

normal: mandarin and lavender
oily: lemon and eucalyptus
dry: rose and camomile

Place a towel over your head and hold your face over the bowl for 2 minutes. This opens the pores, preparing the skin for a face mask.

Note: Don't do this if you are pregnant, have asthma or broken or sensitive skin.

NATURAL FACE SCRUBS/MASKS

Here are three old-fashioned recipes – the first will draw out impurities and the remaining two will tighten your skin.

● Mix 3 tablespoons of oatmeal or porridge oats (not the instant type) with enough milk or yogurt to make a paste. Apply this liberally to your face, avoiding the delicate skin around the eyes. Gently massage your face in small circular motions. Allow the mask to dry completely and then wash it off with warm water. Apply your favourite moisturiser.

● Mix 1–2 tablespoons of oatmeal to a paste with 1 raw egg white.

Apply this to your face and allow it to dry. Rinse with cool water.

● For very dry skin, add a little mayonnaise to the oat and egg white recipe for a smooth finish.

TO TEST LIPSTICK

One of the best places to test lipstick for colour is on the cushion of your finger, where the skin is similar to your lips.

INEXPENSIVE LIP GLOSS

Vaseline is fantastic for soothing cracked lips or for making your lips glossy, either on it's own or over lipstick.

SUNBATHING AT HOME?

Keep the sunscreen and after-sun in the fridge. You've no idea how cooling this is until you've tried it.

PERFUME & SCENT

TO KEEP PERFUME SMELLING

Spray your perfume on to a small ball of cotton wool and pop this into your bra cleavage! The warmth will keep the perfume fresh all day.

FOR BEST-KEPT PERFUME

It may appear glamorous having exotic perfume bottles out in the bedroom or bathroom, but heat and sunlight will spoil the contents. They keep better in a cool drawer or cupboard.

TO CLEAN GLASS SCENT BOTTLES

Fill the bottle with warm water, then add a denture-cleaning tablet. If it doesn't fit into the

bottle, break off a piece of the tablet. Leave overnight and the stains will rinse away.

TO APPLY PERFUME

Put perfume on before you get dressed. Apply it to pulse points on your neck and wrists, and try some behind your knees as well. Don't overdo it; three sprays of perfume and five sprays of eau de toilette are enough. For all-over fragrance, use matching toiletries, including soap and body lotion.

PERFUME STAINS ON FABRIC

Never iron over a perfume stain. The heat may 'set' the mark permanently or remove the colour.

Hand Care

I N EVERYDAY LIFE hands and feet are subject to wear and tear. They need to be pampered and cared for like the rest of your body and face.

SOOTHING CHAPPED HANDS

At bedtime wash your hands in warm water, dry them and rub in glycerine (available with the baking ingredients or from the chemist). If you have a pair of cotton gloves, wear them overnight. Some chemists sell cotton gloves – or those old white gloves are really useful for cleaning silver as well as keeping hand cream on all night!

DISCOLOURED FINGERNAILS?

Soak your fingertips in 600 ml (1 pint) warm water with the juice of 1 lemon.

TO HARDEN FINGERNAILS

Iodine (available at the chemist) is really good for strengthening nails. Dip a cocktail stick into liquid iodine and let a couple of drops drip down into your cuticles. Take care as iodine stains. This is best done at night because it will leave a yellow mark – by the morning the iodine stain will have disappeared.

TO CLEAN DIRTY HANDS

Rub them with Vaseline for 3–4 minutes and then wash in hot soapy water.

TO SMOOTH REALLY ROUGH HANDS

Mix 1 tablespoon of sunflower or vegetable oil, margarine or lard with 1 tablespoon of granulated sugar. Rub this into your hands, vigorously, for about 5 minutes. Rinse well, dry, and apply a little good hand cream. This is a great way to remove fruit stains – especially after picking blackberries.

TO CLEAN NAILS EASILY

Before gardening (or any dirty work), scrape your fingertips over a bar of soap. Soap under the nails brings out dirt afterwards.

TO KEEP HANDS SOFT WHILE GARDENING

Always wear gloves. Before you put them on, rub in a little Vaseline.

SMELLY HANDS AFTER COOKING?

If you are cooking with garlic, onions or fish, your hands can become really smelly. Rub and squeeze your hands around a cut lemon to freshen them up.

TO HELP FADE AGE SPOTS

Try rubbing lemon juice regularly into those brown marks on your hands and legs and you'll find they fade considerably over time.

TO AVOID STICKY LIDS ON NAIL VARNISH POTS

Smear a little Vaseline around the screw threads on the pot.

TO MAKE NAIL VARNISH LAST LONGER

Before varnishing your nails, use cotton wool to rub a little white vinegar or nail varnish remover over them. The acid helps the varnish stick to the nails.

CHOICE OF NAIL FILES

● Crystal nail files are excellent and the

professional choice. They are expensive and made of glass but last forever.
● Emery boards are also good for shortening nails; look out for the washable fine-grained files.
● Metal files are not recommended as they can drag and split the nails.

FOR SHINY NAILS

Invest in a nail buffer. Use every two weeks for a natural shine that looks as good as clear varnish.

TO LOOK AFTER NAILS

● Nail clippers are better than scissors – use them to cut around your nails. Then file to shape (square, curved or pointed, as you like).
● Cuticle remover helps remove dead skin and keep the cuticle healthy. Apply it and use an orange stick wrapped in cotton wool to ease back the cuticle. Then use the pointed end to clean under the nails. The cuticles act as a waterproof seal around your nails, protecting the skin from infection; regular care keeps them soft and healthy.
● Use a nail brush once a day to keep your nails clean.

MANICURE TIPS

Before giving yourself a manicure, dissolve a little liquid soap in a bowl of warm water and soak your nails for about 5 minutes. Scrub them with a nail

brush and dry carefully. When trimmed and tidy, massage in a good hand and nail cream containing vitamin E. To complete your manicure (unvarnished nails), rub a special white pencil under the nail tips.

NAIL VARNISH STAIN?

If your nails are yellow and stained from constantly wearing nail varnish, try rubbing them with half a cut lemon. If this doesn't work try soaking them in warm water with a denture cleaning tablet, or brush on

smoker's toothpaste, leave for 2 minutes and rinse off.

TO STOP NAILS GETTING YELLOW AND STAINED

Always use a base coat under your varnish. Try to leave your nails unvarnished for a few days between each nail painting.

TO MAKE YOUR OWN HAND CREAM

Mix two parts glycerine with one part fresh lemon juice. Massage a little into your hands, before you go to bed at night.

Feet

TO PREVENT BLISTERS

Rub a little vaseline into the tender areas where you may get blisters. This is particularly good before you put on sports socks.

TO HELP DRY UP BLISTERS

Surgical spirit (available at the chemist) brings relief to blistered feet. Soak cotton wool in the spirit and dab it on as required.

FOOTBATH FOR SMELLY FEET

Soak your feet in a bowl of hot water to which you've added 2 tablespoons of bicarbonate of soda.

TO REMOVE TAR

If you get tar on your feet on the beach, rub it off vigorously with toothpaste.

TO MAKE NEW TIGHTS OR STOCKINGS LAST LONGER

Before you wear them for the first time, rinse them in cold water, wring out and place in a freezer bag. Freeze until solid. Let them thaw and dry before wearing them.

LADDERED TIGHTS OR STOCKINGS?

Paint clear nail varnish on both ends of the run when you're wearing the tights or stockings. Keep a small pot in your handbag for emergencies. If you don't have any, try dry soap.

JEWELLERY

RESTORE THE LUSTRE TO PEARLS

Put a little olive oil on a very soft cloth and buff the pearls gently and carefully.

TO RE-STRING BEADS

Use fine nylon hand fishing line to thread the beads. Secure the ends or clasps with a fine knot and seal this by melting the plastic thread over a lighted match. Buy the line from fishing and DIY shops.

TO STOP CHAINS TANGLING

Slide the chain into a drinking straw cut to half the length of the chain, then fasten the clasp on the chain and leave it like this when you're not wearing it.

TO CLEAN IVORY

Ivory is extremely vulnerable and methylated spirit is one of the few substances that will clean without harming it. Dust the ivory first. Then dampen a piece of cotton wool with methylated spirit and gently rub clean. This is good for piano keys too. To clean an ivory comb, soak dental floss in methylated spirit and pull it through the teeth.

TO CLEAN CARVED IVORY

Blow off dust and dirt gently, rather than dusting with a cloth. Then use a cotton bud or soft, old toothbrush dipped in methylated spirit to clean the ivory. Be careful and take your time.

TO CLEAN JEWELLERY

This is a useful basic method but it is NOT suitable for valuable, fragile settings and stones. Fill a small bowl with warm (not hot) water and add a good squeeze of washing-up liquid. Soak the jewellery for about 5 minutes. Take an old soft toothbrush and gently brush each item clean. Use a wooden cocktail stick to get bits out of awkward corners – this is particularly good for earrings. Rinse the jewellery well and drain it on a towel, then dry thoroughly with a hair dryer on a cool setting.

TO REMOVE A TIGHT RING

Even when it does not seem possible to remove a ring, soap works like magic. Work up a really good lather with warm water, keep twisting the ring gently and it will eventually pull off.

SEWING

BASIC SEWING KIT
- a packet of assorted needles
- large darning needle
- a bodkin – a blunt-ended needle for sewing with wool
- thread in various useful colours, such as black, white, navy blue, red, green and cream
- sharp scissors, small and large; don't let anyone use these for any other purpose, especially cutting paper, as they will soon get blunt.

- a good selection of pins, in a pin cushion
- Fasteners: hooks and eyes, and press studs
- a seam ripper (often called a 'quick-un-pick')
- velcro.
- tape measure
- iron-on bonding strip, also known as 'magic' fibre, is useful for taping up hems – great in an emergency, and quick too.

BUTTON BOX

Save spare buttons, beads, fabric samples or other items that come with new clothes. Buttons are expensive to buy. It is sometimes worth cutting buttons off clothes you are throwing out or using as dusters (but not if they're going to a charity shop). Always keep a button – you never know when it will be exactly what you need.

TO MAKE SURE A BUTTON STAYS ON

- For buttons in hardworking places, for example on jeans or overcoats (especially children's), try using dental floss and a darning needle to sew them on. Since the floss is white it will obviously show, but a dab of felt pen will colour it to match the button.
- When it's sewn on, coat the thread in the centre of the button with a little clear nail varnish.

BUTTON EMERGENCIES

This tip is to save time when you are in a hurry. Always keep two needles threaded, with the end of the thread knotted, one with white and one with black thread.

These are ready to go when a button pops off just as you are in a tearing rush – when it's almost impossible to thread a needle.

TO THREAD A NEEDLE WITH WOOL

This can sometimes be difficult, as the ends just seem to bounce out. Try rolling the tip of the wool on a piece of wet soap, rub it between your fingers and you should then be able to thread it through the eye of the needle . Cut the damp tip off afterwards.

TO KEEP SCISSORS SHARP

Cut through a double thickness of tin foil.

QUICK PATCHING

To repair small tears in places that are not exposed to a lot of friction or wear, use iron-on tape on the reverse of the garment. You can usually find some spare material on a hem, or somewhere inside the clothing to back the tape. This will not last forever but it will give a little more life to a favourite garment.

TO QUICK-FIX A BROKEN ZIP

You can sometimes make a temporary rough repair to a broken zip to tide you over. Find the area where the teeth are bent (on either metal or nylon) and make a cut through the zip edge. Re-insert the zipper above the broken teeth, pull it up and then stitch over the cut area below in an overhand stitch to make a zip 'stop'. You will only be able to operate the zip down to this point (the thread stop).

WORKING WITH
COMPUTERS

Computers can make the modern workload pretty light. You can store CDs-worth of songs, albums-worth of pictures, home movies, word-processed documents, entire novels-in-progress and composed music, and books like this on your hard drive. You can communicate with others by email, and even chat with them live. You can download programs to perform every task imaginable. And you can access all of this in an instant, with the click of a mouse.

Once you're online, you can pay your bills, check your bank statements, top up your mobile, renew library books and do your shopping too.

COMPUTER BASICS

CHOOSING A COMPUTER

It is well worth spending some time shopping around and taking advice from friends. Think about what you want to use your computer for and go into the store armed with a list. Be careful about being talked into buying extra peripherals for your computer; printers and scanners often come as part of the package so it is advisable to compare prices before making your final decision. Be very wary of extended warranties, which are rarely worth the cost. Computer hardware and software is constantly being improved and what is new today may be out of date within a matter of months.

WORD PROCESSING

There is a great variety of word processing applications on offer, and what you choose is really dependent on what computer you buy. The program may come as part of a package when you buy your computer and a manual may be enclosed. Increasingly, however, an on-screen manual will be provided instead. If you have no previous experience, it is worth looking through to find out the numerous tricks it has to offer. If no word processing program is included, most programs offer a variety of templates that help you to create professional looking letters, faxes, memos, reports and much more. What's more, you can insert photos, pictures and symbols to your documents to make them more interesting.

How you do this depends on what version you have on your computer. This is the time to turn to the manual or click on the 'help' tab.

INTERNET AND EMAIL

Most computers have a 56k connection to the internet, which you can upgrade to Broadband. 56k is the way to go if you don't use the internet very often.

Pros of 56k

● Cheap, much like making a phone call; you are charged only for the time spent on the phone.

● You can pay a monthly flat rate for unlimited use, by far the best value option.

Cons

● Slower to connect.

● Uses your phone line so that you cannot receive voice calls. (Though you could use BT 'Call answer', which takes a message whilst you're online, and is free). Broadband should be your choice if you like to browse the web for hours on end.

Pros of Broadband

● Most companies provide a free broadband modem when you sign on for their service.

● A monthly charge, so you know that this is all you will be paying.

● Large files, photos and videos can be sent and received quickly.

● No waiting around for web pages to load.

Cons

A monthly charge – if you don't use the internet for a couple of months, you still pay the flat fee.

BROWSING THE WEB

Again, depending on the type of computer you choose, there are a number of different programs and services you can use to search on the internet.

SHOPPING ONLINE

This is an increasingly popular phenomenon and most stores now have their own web page.. You can also open up your own web-based email account so that you can keep in touch with family and friends wherever you may be. Popular email sites are:

www.hotmail.co.uk

www.yahoo.co.uk

www.gmail.com

These providers also offer a search engine facility, in which you can find almost anything. There are many more providers available and some offer search engines and email, some don't. It's up to you who you decide to go with. Popular search engines are:

www. google.com

www.askjeeves.com

PERSONAL DETAILS

Always be careful about supplying personal details on websites, ensure you are dealing with a reputable company that you have heard of, or use the internet to find out more about them. Many people post reviews of companies on websites and if you need help finding something, the search engines can give you assistance if you get stuck.

MUSIC, VIDEO & PHOTOS

CD PLAYERS

CD players read digital information stored on the disk. This digital information can also be stored on your computer hard disk and read from there too. One of the joys of backing up your collection is to make music compilations for family and friends or for yourself.

CD BURNERS

Most machines will now have a CD burner and software built in. Just pop in your blank CD and the program will guide you on your way. You can also compress tracks and load them on to a portable mp3 player (see page 129).

RESTRICTIONS

Warning: copyright restrictions make it illegal to copy anyone else's CDs; by law you must own any music that you copy on to your computer.

VIDEO

In the same way that audio CDs can be stored and played on your computer, so can video files. Digital video recorders can be connected to your computer and the results stored and edited in various dedicated programs. Other programs will help you convert your old video tapes and record them on to DVD.

PHOTOGRAPHS

You can also store digital photos on your computer in virtual albums and email them to relatives and friends. Wedding photographers will make a selection of digital photos available to guests who are sent a link to the photos, enabling them to download the images and view them on screen.

FILESHARING

Once upon a time a program called Napster became very popular with teenagers; a small piece of software put their computers in touch with each other over the internet and allowed them to download and swap their CD collections in mp3 form. This was of course illegal, but it couldn't be stopped, and similar programs quickly flourished. The music industry's response was to set up online stores where you could download songs at a fraction of the price of buying CDs from shops.

STREAMING

Streaming is the term given to sending big chunks of audio and video data downline to your computer. If you miss your favourite radio programme, many popular stations will stream it for up to a week after it aired. If you have a fast enough connection and appropriate software you can also watch TV on your computer, delivered in exactly the same way as cable TV.

HARDWARE & PERIPHERALS

In addition to the software that enables you to perform any of the above functions, there is also an array of hardware that connects to your computer. Some are an integral part of the computer set-up, such as keyboards, monitors and printers; others include flat panels, webcams, digital cameras and mp3 players.

PRINTERS

Printers are very inexpensive these days, but the ink they use isn't.

Questions you should ask when buying a printer include:
● What is the cost per page for colour and black and white printing?
● How much do replacement ink cartridges cost? Can you replace one colour, or do you have to replace the entire colour cartridge when one of the colours runs out? Most desktop printers have black and white and colour cartridges.
● Will your printer still let you print even after it tells you it is

almost out of ink? Some will prompt you to replace cartridges when they are far from empty, and you should be able to ignore this until you are genuinely out of ink. Be assertive on this point.

Peripheral equipment includes :
extra monitors, which enable you to view documents on one screen while working on a document on your main monitor.
flat panels, called tablets, that will digitize anything you draw using a special pen. You can then manipulate and even animate with various dedicated programs, in the same way that most animated films are produced today.
webcams, will link via ?? cables and are normally positioned on top of the monitor, while special software enables you to see on screen anyone you are talking to via their webcams.
digital cameras, so you can store pictures in virtual albums.
mp3 players, which you can fill with a selection of the music you have stored on your computer and listen while on the train, walking or at the gym.

OOPS...

What used to take a long time can now be done quickly. But if you can access all of this technological power at the click of a mouse, it pretty much follows you can lose it just as quickly. You can take your computer to a big store where someone will 'tut tut' at you and charge you to retrieve any data that's recoverable, but generally it means starting again. The same is true if you have a power cut or a lightning strike or other unexpected power surge; this can completely wipe your hard drive and everything on it. The bottom line is: if you have stuff on your computer you don't want to lose, do the following.
● Save regularly while working on your document.
● Invest in a power surge protector.
● Perform regular backups of all of your data.

BACKUPS
Backups need explanation. You can buy dedicated programs to automate the process, scheduling backups of specified files at a given time each day or week, or you can manually copy data folders whenever you remember, or when you have just done something of vital importance. There are various media you can copy your data on to, including
● memory sticks
● CDs and DVDs
● external hard drives

MEMORY STICKS
Memory sticks are small and cheap, and can be used to carry work from one computer to another. If you finish at the office and want to do more work at home they're ideal. They're the size of key fobs and most of them can actually be used to put your

keys on. There's not much more to them than a USB plug, but the larger capacity sticks will store more than a CDs worth of data.

CDS

CDs are the smallest form of recommended backup for all of your data. The standard capacity is 700MB, with recordable DVDs extending this to 4.7GB, some six and a half times as much. Some of the less expensive new computers will write CDs but not DVDs, but you can buy an add-on DVD writer fairly cheaply.

EXTERNAL HARD DRIVES

External hard drives connect to your computer via USB or a similar – but generally faster – connection standard called Firewire. You could back up your hard drive in its entirety by buying an external drive the same size as your hard drive. If you lose any of the program files, or they become corrupted, you can quite simply reinstall them.

POWER SURGES

The only problem with external hard drives as backup solutions is that if you are hit by some power surge or lightning strike that takes out your computer and destroys your hard disk it could well do that to your external drive too.

SERIOUS BACK-UP

Tape drives are a frequent big-business solution; rather than using filing cabinets full of paper copies, data records can be archived and backed up daily or even more frequently on industrial-strength tape systems. After a period of a week, a month or six months the tapes will be reused, but you can set the level of security yourself, keeping copies for as long as you think useful.

Online storage is a useful and secure solution. You can use your internet connection to zap your data downline to a specialist firm as regularly as you care, but it can be expensive, so check out the costs and also the guarantees.

SECURITY

FIREWALL

If you are connected to the internet in any way at all, whether through a modem or high-speed broadband connection, you are potentially open to interference with your data, personal details, hardware and software, in fact anything you keep on your computer. If it's there, it can be accessed by someone connected to the internet at the same time.

Data can be read and copied, modified or entirely wiped by a third party. To prevent unauthorised access to your data you should install a firewall program. A firewall will prevent other computer users accessing the files on your computer.

VIRUSES

Viruses are generally sent by email, as attachments. If you open them, they can do a number of bad things to your computer, such as wiping your hard drive and automatically sending themselves to everyone in your address book. Anti-virus software checks the contents of your drive for files of this sort. You'll receive updates via your internet connection as soon as a virus is identified, so that your program can easily spot it. The safest option is never to open attachments from unknown sources.

HOME OFFICE TIPS

If you are going to spend much time in your home office, it's important to make sure you're comfortable. If your chair, monitor, keyboard and mouse are not right, you could end up with back pain, eye strain or repetitive strain injury (RSI), or all three!

THE ERGONOMIC KEYBOARD AND MOUSE

A number of keyboard designs have been developed to make life easier on your body. The most common is a fixed-angle split design to increase comfort in fingers and wrists. New developments include keyboards designed for one-handed typists.

The mouse has been redesigned again and again, especially for those people who have hand and wrist problems. As ever, you can find the latest research and developments on the internet.

WRIST RESTS FOR KEYBOARDS

These cover hard surfaces to give more comfort. They support the wrists and encourage a neutral wrist position.

A combined mouse pad and wrist rest also provides comfort and support for your wrist.

CHAIRS

Get yourself a really good, fully adjustable chair. DON'T use a kitchen chair. You'll need:
● an adjustable backrest and armrest
● a swivel base
● a comfortably cushioned, height-adjustable seat.

MONITORS

Don't lean to one side to view the monitor; set it square on to look straight ahead when working. Don't lower your face or crane upwards to view the monitor – this is a major cause of neck pain. Position your monitor and then adjust the seat height accordingly. Adjust the brightness of the monitor according to instructions to prevent eye strain.

HOLDING BACK CHAOS

Drill a hole in the back of your desk to pull through electrical cables. Tidy away cables from your peripherals under and behind the desk using cheap mug hooks from a DIY store. You may be able to hang your computer hardware under your desk with special holders to free up much-needed desk and floor space.

CARS
& BIKES

This section is not everything you ever wanted to know about cars, bicycles and motorcycles, but it will give your some pointers on how to maintain your 'wheels' and get the best performance from them, as well as basic information about laws and safety precautions and a few hints on how to survive car journeys with children.

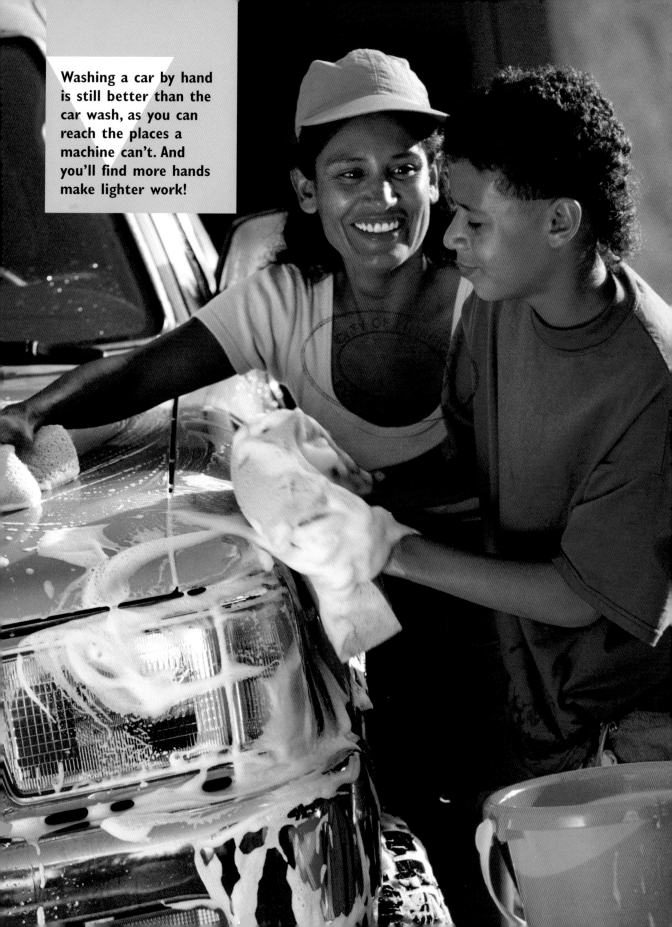

Washing a car by hand is still better than the car wash, as you can reach the places a machine can't. And you'll find more hands make lighter work!

CLEANING YOUR CAR

TO CLEAN CHROME AND HEADLIGHTS
A good rub with bicarbonate of soda on a damp cloth works wonders.

TO REMOVE NASTY SMELLS FROM THE CAR ASHTRAY
Put a teaspoon of bicarbonate of soda into the bottom of the ashtray. It may not deter smokers but it will neutralize the smell.

TO GET RID OF GREASY MARKS ON THE WINDSCREEN
Make a thin paste of bicarbonate of soda and water and give the windscreen a good rub. Rinse well.

TO REMOVE FLIES AND INSECTS FROM THE WINDSCREEN
Use a green household scourer, warm water and washing up liquid. The scourer is non-abrasive and will not harm the glass.

TO REMOVE UNWANTED 'GIFTS' THAT BIRDS LEAVE ON THE CAR
Take some waterless (aqueous) hand cream, and with an old rag work it well into the affected area. Let it sit for about 5 minutes and the mark should rub off easily.

TO REMOVE ROAD TAR
Soak an old rag with linseed oil (available from hardware and DIY stores) and apply liberally to the tarred area, leave it to soak for a few minutes, then wipe off with the oily rag. Make sure that you throw the rag away immediately.

TO REMOVE NASTY OR MUSTY SMELLS FROM THE INTERIOR
Put some cat litter into a nylon stocking, or half a pair of tights, tie a knot in the end to seal. You can place these out of sight, under the seat or in the boot.

TO REVITALIZE PAINTWORK ON AN OLDER CAR
"T Cut" or "Mer" polish should bring back some of the colour and shine. Read the manufacturers instructions carefully, and use lots of elbow grease. This works especially well on red paint.

CAR WASH
Going to the car wash is great for a quick clean and polish, but it doesn't get into all the nooks and crannies. Remember to close all the windows and the sunroof, and retract the radio aerial.

WASHING AND RINSING YOUR CAR BY HAND
Doing it by hand is still the most effective way to get a car really clean. A hosepipe really helps and you can get various attachments with brushes that fit over the end. Rinse well, using the hose, and buff dry with a chamois leather.
● Always make sure before you start that the cloths, brushes etc. are completely clean and grit free,

the tiniest piece of grit could completely ruin the paintwork.
● A really good idea is to get the children involved, they will love the water, the soap and the hosepipe, and when they get older you can encourage them to do it alone for pocket money!

BASIC CAR MAINTENANCE

BONNET RELEASE
Almost every make of car has its own bonnet opening device. Look in your car manual to find where it is. Some have a lock on the bonnet, and you just insert the ignition key and "hey presto".

OPENING THE BONNET
Once you have released the bonnet, there is always a safety catch lever to undo. In my experience these are always difficult to locate and are invariably oily and dirty. Persevere; they are usually located in the gap between the bonnet and radiator.

ENGINE OIL
It makes good sense to have the engine oil changed once a year when the car is serviced, but do check it regularly, especially before a long journey and if your car is more than 10 years old.

CHECKING OIL
Make sure the engine is cold and the car is parked on the level.

DIPSTICK LOCATION
Check your manual to see where the dipstick is located, then take it out and wipe it clean (kitchen paper is good for this). You will see that there are 'max.' and 'min.' markers on it. Re-dip the stick, pushing it in as far as it will go, then pull it out carefully. Your oil level needs to be about halfway between the two markers.

TOPPING UP OIL
If you need more oil, consult your manual for the type, and buy a good proprietary brand. A plastic funnel is useful for pouring and preventing spills on the engine.

AUTOMATIC TRANSMISSIONS
If you own an automatic car you will also need to keep an eye on the 'automatic transmission fluid' This is an oil that is especially for automatic gear boxes, and can be bought from motoring shops.

BRAKE FLUID
You may need to top up with this yourself occasionally. A light on the dashboard should warn you that it needs to be done.

WARNING LIGHTS
If a light suddenly appears on the dashboard, stop at once and check the manual, which should always be kept in your car.

DIESEL ENGINES

If you own a diesel vehicle, you won't have to top up the oil yourself, but the garage will need to drain and change the engine oil regularly. Check the manual for details of when it should be done, usually every 10,000 miles or so.

RADIATOR CARE

The car radiator or coolant reservoir needs Antifreeze or Coolant to stop the water freezing in winter. The garage will put some in when servicing, but you should check levels as well.

FILL TO LEVELS

The coolant reservoir has a min. and max. level. Fill to the max. with the makers recommended water/antifreeze mix. If you have an older car you may not have a separate coolant container; in which case it goes straight into the top of the radiator tank.

WINDSCREEN WASH

Do keep your windscreen washer water topped up. You may think it's unnecessary in summer, but if the road is dusty or there are lots of flies about you'll be cursing the fact that the bottle is empty.

Use clean water to fill the container. The kettle is good for pouring as it has a spout, or use a funnel (but not the one you use for oil) Add a few drops of screen wash as well, although I always use washing up liquid.

CHECK TYRES

Don't forget to check your tyres regularly and have the wheels 'balanced'. The garage will give you some advice when the car is serviced. Tyres can wear unevenly and be dangerous, especially on wet roads; and they may be so worn that they are illegal.

TYRE PRESSURES

It is also important to check the tyre pressures regularly. Under-inflated tyres are dangerous, because they can ruin a car's handling as well as its ability to perform economically.

Tyre pressures can be done at the garage or service station, using the pressure pump. However, many of these don't work properly or are difficult to operate so ask for advice on your first visit.

Tyre pressures vary from car to car so look in your manual for the details. (It makes a difference to tyre pressure if you're towing or carrying heavy weights.) Tyre pressures for back and front are sometimes on the inside of the drivers door for quick reference.

TO PREVENT A BATTERY CORRODING

To stop corrosion on a non-sealed battery, rub a little Vaseline around the dry terminals.

KEEP THE BATTERY TOPPED UP

Keep your battery (if it is non-sealed) topped up with water, but never use tap water. Use distilled (ionized) water, which can be bought in any garage.

A HEALTHY BATTERY

Do keep your battery clean, fully topped up, and replace it on a regular basis – your car will thank you for it!

AIR CONDITIONING

If you have air conditioning, remember that it needs to be run regularly to keep it 'happy'. On cold winter mornings you can use it on hot, for a fast de-mist.

FAULTY BRAKE OR HEADLIGHT?

If you suspect you might have a faulty brake light or headlight (think how many drivers you see with only one rear or headlight), and there's no one to help you, test your lights against a wall or garage door at night.

BREAKDOWN SERVICES

Join a breakdown service (The AA or RAC). Even if you know how to change a tyre, it's almost impossible to remove the bolts yourself these days as they're tightened by machine in the factory or workshop.

HOME START

Consider getting cover at home as well, since the basic service does not usually include "home start" and you could be caught out, as I once was, if your car won't start or a tyre has gone flat overnight.

RELAY

If you do a lot of mileage, it is also worth considering having "relay". This is a service that will bring you and your car back home from anywhere in the UK. My exhaust once fell off on the motorway at midnight! I was whisked home with the car in no time at all.

MOT

If your car is three or more years old it will need an MOT test. When (and if) it passes you will receive a certificate which must be presented when you tax your car. If you loose your MOT certificate you can obtain a copy from the garage where the car was tested.

BEWARE!

Don't keep anything heavy on the back shelf. In the event of a crash, these items could shoot forward, harming you or your passengers.

GARAGE PARKING

To prevent bumping your car in a tight garage, attach an old tyre to the end wall, It will act as a buffer, in the same way that fenders work on boats.

COLD WEATHER

FROZEN LOCKS?

Try sticking thick masking tape over the locks at night, this prevents the moisture getting in.
● If you keep your car in the garage and have an electric plug handy, try using a hair dryer on frozen locks, no closer than 15 cm (6 in) though. Warning: be careful if you have an electric locking device as you risk damaging it.
● WD40 (penetrating oil) is excellent for defrosting locks. Spray the lock and insert the plastic tube into the lock barrel and give a good squirt. Insert the key and wiggle it from side to side until the lock opens.

TO PREVENT A FROZEN/SNOWY WINDSCREEN IN THE MORNING
Place an old towel, blanket or newspaper on your windscreen overnight and secure it with the windscreen wipers.

ICE ON THE WINDOWS
Buy an ice scraper and a can of de-icer spray. Make sure you keep these in your car as one day you'll need them. Eco-friendly products are available in plastic bottles.

WHAT TO DO IF YOU BREAKDOWN

GET OFF THE ROAD
The first thing to remember if you do breakdown is to get your car out of the way of traffic. Try to move it to the left (or hard shoulder on a motorway).

BEWARE OF TRAFFIC
Only 7 per cent of breakdowns happen on the motorway, but if this happens to you, get all the passengers out of the car and behind the barrier for protection.

Stationary cars have been known to be hit on the hard shoulder.

A WOMAN ALONE
If you are a woman on your own the breakdown services will usually make you a special case and come as quickly as possible. You may feel safer inside your car.

HAZARD WARNING LIGHTS
Alert other motorists to the fact that you've broken down by using your hazard warning lights. You should be aware of where they are and how to switch them on.

WARNING TRIANGLE
You could also use a Warning Triangle. These are not obligatory in the UK but are required in most of Europe, so it could be a wise investment.

INFORMING THE BREAKDOWN SERVICES
When you phone your breakdown service they will want to know the basic details of the problem, so have a quick look around the car before you phone and note any noises, smells or emissions.

USEFUL THINGS TO KEEP IN YOUR BOOT

- an old blanket or rug is a good idea if you breakdown and need to lie on the ground to look under the car – or just keep warm.
- a shovel
- warm clothes
- water to drink
- the phone number and details of your breakdown service
- a basic First Aid kit
- a good torch
- a detailed map or road guide
- a can of tyre foam, which can be squirted into a punctured tyre and will keep it inflated long enough to get you to a garage (available at motor accessory stores).

CAR TRIPS WITH CHILDREN

'Are we nearly there?' This is every parent's nightmare. I can remember saying it myself, and being so bored on car journeys. Here are a few suggestions for passing the time.

I WENT TO THE SHOPS

This is a simple but fun memory game, using the alphabet. The first player says 'I went to the shop and bought something beginning with A (e.g. Apple)'. The next player says 'I went to the shop and bought an apple and something beginning with B (e.g. Bath)', and so on through the alphabet.

CITY OR COUNTRY ALPHABET

The first player starts with, say, London and the the next player has to name a place beginning with the last letter – in this case N, and so it goes on.

I SPY (WITH MY LITTLE EYE)

The age-old car and train journey game. Try using colours instead of letters for younger children.

QUIET GAMES

This really is rather clever! Get the children to sit as quietly as possible for as long as possible; the winner should receive a small prize (i.e. a favourite chocolate bar or choosing the next pit stop).

Hand held computer games can be quiet too!

LISTEN OR SINGALONG

Play a tape or CD of children's stories or songs to suit the age range, or something like The Beatles that Mum and Dad can appreciate too. Nursery rhymes are a good idea for young children although they may drive you mad on a long drive!

WHERE DO LORRIES COME FROM?

Guess where the cars and lorries are from by their 'plates'. These can be checked in The AA Book. There are many lorries on the road now from all over Europe; you could try to guess what they are carrying too.

FOOD AND DRINK

Do make sure you have plenty of cold drinks, in a cool box, wet wipes, tissues, sweets, fruit (grapes and bananas are good car food) or take a picnic box or bag (see page 165-169 for ideas). We all know how overpriced and awful most motorway service station food is.

STOP ON THE WAY

If it is a particularly long journey, (London/Manchester to West Cornwall, for example) try breaking the journey half way to stay with friends or at a B&B or motel. If you leave on a Friday afternoon, you'll arrive on Saturday reasonably refreshed and rested.

YOUR BICYCLE

SUSTRANS

According to 'Sustrans', a charity that helped create the National Cycle Network, there are 10,000 miles of cycle routes around the UK. These routes are clearly signposted, safe for cyclists, and attractive to use. One third of the routes are traffic-free areas, such as canal towpaths and disused railway lines. To find out about 'Sustrans' cycle routes in your area:www.sustrans.org.uk

THE WAY TO TRAVEL

In 2005/6 local authorities outside London expect to spend about £46 million – a huge investment – so that the cycling successes in some cities can roll out elsewhere. Now is the time to "Get cycling". It's fun, fast, green and healthy!

START CYCLING

CYCLISTS' HIGHWAY CODE

A good start is the Highway Code, which gives all the details of what cyclists are obliged to do by law.

HELMETS

Buy a good quality helmet that fits your head properly; it protects your head and could save your life if you are involved in an accident.
● It is not yet compulsory in the UK to wear a helmet, but it is advisable. It's the law in Spain, Australia and New Zealand and is mandatory for UK postmen and for children, whether on their own bike or the back of an adult's.

LIGHTS

By law, cyclists riding at night must have lights fitted to the front and back of their bikes; not using then can incur a fine of £30.

REFLECTORS

These must be fitted to pedals and to the back of your bike. You can also buy them on belts and armbands. Be safe and be seen.

FLUORESCENT CLOTHING

This is a good idea as it makes it easier for other road users to see you at night. You can buy stick-on reflective stripes, shoulder pads, and reflective gloves too.

PANNIERS AND BACKPACKS

You could invest in panniers (fixed containers) for your bike, or choose a rucksack that is comfortable and light for cycling.

BICYCLE REPAIR KIT

Make sure you have a small emergency tool kit with the appropriate spanners and tyre levers for your bike, a puncture repair kit, a pump and maybe a spare inner tube.

WET WEATHER GEAR

Keep light wet-weather clothing in your rucksack or pannier.

FOOT/SHOE CLIPS

If you want to get the maximum power and push from your bike these are recommended. You can buy specialist cycling shoes with a lightweight spike on the sole that clips to the pedal.

Older style toe clips are still available on some bikes; this type of foot/toe clip is advisable for hill cycling.

SADDLE POSITION

The recommended saddle position for a male bike with a cross-bar is: when your feet are flat on the ground your crutch should just skim the crossbar. When you cycle, your foot (with leg fully extended) should just miss the ground. Quick release saddles, which make seat adjustment easier, are available.

TYPES OF BIKE

It is up to you whether you choose the old-fashioned 'sit up and beg', straight handle bar bike or the more racy lean-over style. Mountain bikes are ridden upright (mostly off-road) and are nearer to the ground than road bikes.

SAFE CYCLING

It is wise to cycle single file and to avoid bunching in small groups. Be wary of cycling on pavements and of people opening car doors, observe red lights and use cycle lanes when they are provided. Keep speed under control, be aware of other traffic, and always look out and listen for walkers, fellow cyclists and horse riders.

CHILDREN

Make sure that children are aware of road safety before they venture out for the first time. Check to see if the school or local council runs cycling proficiency tests.

CYCLING PROFICIENCY

Cycling Proficiency has a successor called National Standard for Cycle Training, with three separate levels:
● Beginner and basic cycling skills, 7 years and upwards
● Introduction to on-road cycling, 9-10 years and over
● Advanced cycling, for very busy roads

SECURITY

Fear of theft is one of the biggest deterrents to growth in cycling. Here are some general tips:
● Always lock a bike, even if you are only leaving it for a few moments, and never leave it in an isolated place.
● Secure bikes to a proper bike stand, or robust street furniture with a stout chain/clamp and a strong D lock. You may invalidate your insurance if you do not secure your bike adequately.
● Lock bicycles through the frame, secure or remove the wheels and also the lights, pump, and quick-release saddle, if you have one.

● Removable wheels are available that have a double setting to release the brake pads, which makes taking off the wheel easier.

● Remember that half of cycle thefts happen at home.

● Your bicycle will have an individual frame number, usually located at the bottom of the seat tube or stamped on the underside of the bottom bracket. Make a note of this and keep it somewhere safe; the police will need it if your bike is stolen.

● Extra security can be gained by having your postcode, house number and a personal code etched into the frame. Most good cycle dealers offer this service, or ask at your local police station.

BIKES BY RAIL

Bikerail is a website that has information on coach and rail services that carry bikes throughout the UK: Log on to www.ctc.org.uk

BIKE INSURANCE

Consider taking insurance cover against injury to yourself and to others in case of an accident.

CLEANING & MAINTENANCE

Never clean your bicycle with a high-pressure washer as the pressure of the water will wash the grease from the bearings.

ECO-FRIENDLY CLEANING

Various special cleaning agents are available to clean your bike. For environmental reasons it is advisable to use products that are biodegradable.

DAILY RUB DOWN

Always clean your bike after a ride, particularly if you're not going to use it the next day. A product called 'Muck Off' makes light of cleaning and is environmentally sound.

Give a good general rub down of all moving parts with an oily rag kept specially for the purpose.

WHEELS AND TYRES

Check that the spokes are tight, and that your tyres are correctly inflated and are not perishing.

OILING GEARS AND CHAIN

Special attention must be made to the gear mechanism, which needs to be oiled with either '3-in-one' oil (good value), a PTFE or similar lubricant. Apply the same oil to the chain. Turn the bike upside down on the saddle and turn the peddles whilst applying the oil to the chain. This should be done regularly as it rusts easily.

BRAKES

Check them regularly to make sure they're working; you don't want to be halfway down a hill when you discover they're faulty!

LIGHTS

Regularly check the batteries, as you may have to use lights on a wet day, even in summer.

BELL

Ensure that you always have a working bell.

IF YOUR BIKE HASN'T BEEN USED FOR A WHILE

If you don't cycle daily, and sometimes leave your bike for two or more weeks at a time, you will need to re-lubricate the parts before you take it out again.

STORING YOUR BIKE

If you're not using your bike for a while, it's a good idea to store it upside down to protect the tyres, or hang it from securely mounted, padded hooks.

GET IT CHECKED

If you haven't cycled for a while, get your bike checked by a local cycle shop before you use it again.

HELP WITH PROBLEMS

Either consult the manual if you have one, or pop into a cycle shop if you need professional help.

YOUR MOTORBIKE

This section is not aimed at bikers who own large, powerful motorbikes, but contains a few basic tips for small motorbike, moped and scooter users.

TRAINING AND TESTS

The starting point for all Learner drivers is the Compulsory Basic Training (CBT) certificate. This course was introduced in 1990 to help reduce high accident rates amongst inexperienced riders.

● All Learner motorcycle, scooter and moped riders must complete a CBT course before riding on the road. Only then will a provisional licence be issued.

● When you take your test (not CBT) a radio receiver will be fitted to your belt, and an earpiece will be fitted into your helmet.

● The examiner will follow you, either on a motorbike or in a car. After the test, the examiner will ask you questions.

● Until you pass your test, you may only ride 125cc bikes. After this, the size depends on your age and various other details (see Licences, page 144).

● A moped is a motorcycle that cannot go faster than 50 mph and cannot have an engine over 50cc.

ROAD TAX FOR MOTORBIKES, SCOOTERS AND MOPEDS

● Under 150cc £15 pa
● 151cc – 400cc £30 pa
● 401cc – 600cc £45 pa
● All other bikes £60 pa

Motorbikes only need a licence plate on the rear, and the characters can be smaller than on other road vehicles.

MOTOR SCOOTERS

Scooters (invented by the Italians in 1947) have step-through frames, the rider does not actually straddle any part of the engine, which is located under the seat near the rear wheel. They have smaller wheels than motorbikes and, typically, smaller engines.

LICENCES

There are hugely complicated rules and details about motorbike licences for car drivers, for various age groups, and for the size of bike you may ride. To check this out go to: www.dsa.gov.uk, The Driving Standards Agency or phone 0115 901 2500.

CLEANING & MAINTENANCE

These are only basic tips. Always refer to your manual and take advice from the local motorbike shop. Keeping your bike in tip-top condition is a priority.

BATTERY

It takes 10–15 minutes riding at 50/60 mph to recharge what you use starting up the bike. Persistent short journeys and slow runs will deteriorate your battery.

● A motorbike will place a drain on the battery even when it is not in use. If you are storing your bike over the winter, or for longer than 6 weeks, it's a good idea to remove the battery.

● To store the battery, fully charge it and put it into a safe, dry place – not near any electric fires or where it may freeze.

BATTERY CHARGERS

Use a charger suitable for your type of battery, it should give a greater output than the battery voltage, so check your manual.

TYRES

Tyres connect you to the road, so it's essential that you have the correct type.

● Make sure you have the right tyre pressure for your bike. You should have them fitted and correctly balanced by a professional, then check the pressures regularly.

CHAIN DRIVE

Keep an eye on the chain; it needs oiling regularly and to be kept free of dust. Refer to the manual for information on this.

CHECKLIST

Before going out on a ride, have a quick 2-minute check of the following:

● all the lights
● brakes
● tyre pressures
● horn

SAFETY & CLOTHING

Thirty to thirty-five per cent of car drivers involved in accidents with motorbikes claim that they didn't see them coming. Knowing your bike, knowing your ability and knowing what's going on around you are the essential tools for safety. You need to anticipate what other road users are doing.

REFLECTIVE CLOTHING

Black leather is great, but do add a brightly coloured, reflective waistcoat, reflective armbands, reflective gloves, or a high visibility belt. You can also buy stick-on reflective stripes.

EXTRA PROTECTION

Clothing should have extra thick contact protection on various parts of the body, like elbows, knees, shoulders, hips and back. You can buy special jackets with 'plastic ribs' in the back to protect your spine.

ALL-WEATHER GEAR

Clothing should be a snug fit and have ventilation points. Consider a PVC over-suit for wet weather, and leather boots.

HELMETS

Always buy a new helmet, never secondhand, and spend as much as you can afford. They have tough outer skins and are designed to absorb impact. Helmets are made from fibre glass or polycarbonate.

● Helmets must conform with many UK safety standards, so make sure you buy from a reputable shop and that you get one that fits you comfortably.

HEADLIGHTS

These need to be on when you are using the bike. With most modern bikes, the lights come on automatically with the ignition.

A GOOD LOCK

Locks can be large and expensive, but you definitely need one or more, with a big chain that goes through the wheel or wheels.

TO DETER EASY THEFT

A specialist motor cycle cover, thrown over the bike, can act as a deterrent and a delaying tactic, because it's a hassle to remove it.

SCOOTER LOCK

Locks for scooters need a chain that will fit over the seat (where the engine is kept). This makes it almost impossible to break open the seat cover.

INSURANCE

Some insurance companies dictate strict security procedures, so check them out. You may find that if you don't have a garage for your bike you'll be asked to secure the bike with a chain and 'bolt eye', mounted in concrete on the ground.

THE GREAT
OUTDOORS

Whether you have a pocket-handkerchief patio, large vegetable and flower gardens or fancy the idea of leasing an allotment, you'll find all sorts of helpful hints and tips in this chapter. Not only is there information about your own patch but also advice on wild food, picnics and barbecues. From vegetables, herbs and flowers to feeding the birds or getting rid of garden pests, find out what you need to make the most of the great outdoors.

An allotment is a beautiful thing. If you don't have enough space in your garden to grow vegetables, you can lease the land for a small amount a year and get growing.

GENERAL GARDEN TIPS

NATURAL FERTILIZERS

The following is a selection of natural fertilizers for the garden.

- Crushed egg shells – work them into the soil well.
- Bury used coffee grounds to provide acid in alkaline soil.
- Water from a fish tank or goldfish bowl is full of nutrients – use it on outdoor pot plants.
- Save the water from boiled noodles or pasta. Leave it to cool and use to water plants, they love the starch in the water.

EGG-BOX SEED TRAYS

Use cardboard egg boxes as seed trays. Plant 2–3 seeds in each cup. When they come through, pinch out the weaker ones and let the strong one grow on. When ready to plant out, cut the boxes into individual cups and put them straight into the garden. The plant roots will grow undisturbed and the cardboard will gradually disintegrate.

TOILET-ROLL PLANTERS

I understand that the cardboard middles from toilet rolls cannot be taken into school for children to use in crafts, so this is a new use for them. They are particularly good for growing peas, beans and sweet peas. During the winter, save the cardboard centres from toilet rolls. Stand them upright, fill with compost and plant a single germinated seed in each earth-filled tube. The cardboard roll can be planted in soil and will slowly disintegrate.

TO GERMINATE PEA, BEAN AND SWEET PEA SEEDS

Soak the seeds in cold water for 24 hours. This is called 'chitting' and helps the tough outer shell of the seed to break open, which in turn speeds up the germination.

TO MAKE PLANT LABELS

Cut the bottom out of a plastic yogurt pot and then cut the side of the pot into strips. Use a permanent marker pen to write on the strips of plastic, leaving room for pushing the ends into the soil. Hey presto!

TO FIT A GARDEN HOSE

To help push the hose on to a tap or into a fitting try rubbing the inside of the hose with some soap. This eases it on the tap or fitting and the soap will quickly dry afterwards.

TO MAKE BIRD SCARERS

Unwanted CDs are fantastic for this. Thread string through their middles and tie the CDs on a stick or bamboo pole, where they will twist in the wind, catch the light and sparkle.

SQUIRREL-PROOF BIRD FEEDERS

To stop the squirrels getting all the peanuts you put out for the birds, look out for small feeders that fix on the window with plastic suction pads. These can be located in the middle of a window where there is nowhere for squirrels to hang on. The window pane may get a little messy but the pleasure of seeing the birds close up makes it worthwhile.

FEEDING THE BIRDS

If using bread, try brown or wholemeal. I whiz the crusts, a couple of the last slices and some peanuts in the food processor to make it easier for the birds to eat. In very cold weather I add a few porridge oats as well. It's best to put the mixture on a high bird table to discourage the local cats from stalking the birds.

TO BEAT SLUGS AND SNAILS

There are various tips for stopping slugs and snails eating your favourite plants and vegetables.
- Try sprinkling bran around your plants. Slugs are attracted to it but it kills them. It also attract snails: they will assemble around it making it easy to collect them.
- Bury a plastic cup to the rim in soil near your plants and half fill it with beer or lager. The slugs will drink the beer, fall in and drown.
- Sprinkle gravel or crushed egg shells around your favourite plants, which you know the snails and slugs love. They do not like to crawl over gravel – try imagining how uncomfortable it must be!

TO MAKE TIES FOR TALL PLANTS

This is useful for tomato plants and tall or large perennials. Old tights and stockings make great ties – they are strong and flexible yet soft enough not to cut into the plants' stems

TO STAKE TALL PERENNIALS

Always do this early. You can bet your life that if you think 'I must do that tomorrow', that night there will be high winds and your favourite plants will be blown to the ground. Use bamboo canes and string or try some of the new propriety products on offer in the garden centre. The other advantage of staking plants early is that they grow over or around the stakes to hide them effectively.

TO DETER GREENFLY ON ROSES

Try planting garlic cloves around each rose bush. This may not be 100 per cent effective, but it does help and you do have the bonus of harvesting freshly grown garlic.

TO DISCOURAGE MOLES

Human hair is an irritant to moles! If you cut your children's or family's hair save it for this or ask the hairdresser for a bag of clippings. Remove the mole hill and you will see the hole where the mole has pushed up the soil. Push some hair into this and – hopefully – the mole will move on. The soil from the mole hill is fantastic with potting compost for potting and planting – you will find that it has become soft and aerated by the mole's digging.

TO GET RID OF WEEDS ON PATHS AND PATIOS

This is useful for those weeds that grow through the cracks in your drive and patio. Add half a cup of salt to a gallon of cold water and stir until it dissolves. Water the weeds well with the salt solution.

TO PREVENT WEEDS GROWING IN CRACKS
Sprinkle dry salt directly into the actual crack or hole; this also works well in the area around the edge of your house.

TO REMOVE RUST FROM GARDEN TOOLS
Use a stiff wire brush to remove the rust and then scrape over the dull edges with a metal file. Rub in some linseed oil.

TO SMOOTH WOODEN HANDLES ON GARDEN TOOLS
This remove splinters and conditions the wood. Rub rough handles with light sand paper and then rub in some linseed oil. This will protect the wood and stop it splitting and cracking again.

TO CLEAN PLASTIC PATIO FURNITURE
Grimy plastic garden furniture will come clean really quickly when you give it a good scrub with a solution of washing soda. Allow $1/2$ cup soda to 600 ml (1 pint) water.

THE VEGETABLE GARDEN

STARTING A VEGETABLE PLOT
There are a few things to plan when you start a proper vegetable plot. For example, if you have lots of space or an allotment, mark your plot into 1.2-metre (4 foot) wide growing beds. This is a good, manageable size.
● Start a compost heap.
● Work out a planting rotation plan to keep crops moving around the plot, rather than planting the same type of vegetable in the same place year after year; this helps to prevent pests and diseases from taking hold.

Peas require soil that has been well dug with manure. In dry weather they should be mulched and well supported with sticks or stakes, allowing good space for the pods to develop on the plants.

Broad beans enjoy soil that has been dug deeply and well manured. Plant the beans 15 cm (6 in) apart. Pick out the top shoots when the lower pods are set and you will get well-filled pods throughout the season.

French beans need a sunny position, protection from the wind and lots of watering. They also need to be picked regularly while they are young and tender.

Runner Beans require deeply dug soil, lots of manure and huge amounts of water. Put your bean poles in early. Set them deep and secure them well – you will not believe how heavy the plants become when laden with beans. You can also grow runner beans on a tripod of bamboo canes set amongst flowers or in a large tub.

Grow tomatoes in your greenhouse, in a growbag or in the garden. Don't bother growing from seed (unless you are an expert), but buy small plants. Gardener's Delight is one of the best varieties to try the first time: These are tiny tomatoes, about the size of walnuts, very sweet and juicy, and they're not available in the shops. Nip out the growing tip at the top of the plant when you have five or six healthy looking trusses (fruit-bearing side shoots). Water and feed the plants well.

TO PROTECT MARROWS AND ONIONS

During the summer months, while they are still growing, place a

house tile or flat stone under marrow and onion plants. This keeps them dry during the day and warm at night.

TO STORE APPLES AND PEARS

If you have fruit trees, pick the fruit when it's ripe. Check each fruit to ensure there is no bruising or insect infestation – it takes just one or two dodgy fruit to develop mould and spread this to the rest. Find a cool, airy, dark place to store them – a good secure shed that is not invaded by mice is ideal. Lay out the fruit on newspaper, not letting them touch each other. Look out for cardboard fruit trays with indentations, thrown away in the greengrocers, as they are useful for laying out fruit. Airy plastic racks or ventilated cardboard boxes are good for stacking. If you store it well, you should be able to continue eating the fruit until the following spring.

THE HERB GARDEN

TO POSITION A HERB GARDEN

Think of the times when the it's wet, cold or both and plant herbs as near as is possible to your kitchen door. Then, armed with scissors, you can just nip outside and cut what you need.

SELECTING HERBS

Those mentioned here make up a good selection of basic herbs to

start off your plot. For using herbs in cooking, see pages 45-47. If you're an expert, try growing herbs from seed; if not, just buy plants. Don't buy herbs for the garden from the supermarket as they are primarily bred to grow on your windowsill for little more than a week. Most herbs prefer sunny, well-drained soil and not much feeding.

CHIVES

Interestingly the history of chives goes back 5,000 years – the Romans brought them to Britain. They are easy to grow and should be watered during dry spells as their small bulbous roots are close to the surface. Cut the flower heads off regularly (small purple pompoms), otherwise they will run to seed and the stalks will become tough. They live for a long time and enjoy a good feed; otherwise their tips go yellow. Cutting can continue until the first frosts, when they will die back and reappear in early spring.

MARJORAM (OREGANO)

The Romans also brought this herb to Britain. They considered it to be a symbol of peace and happiness. There are many types so be sure to buy a plant that is a perennial. The summer flowers are a great attraction for bees. Plant in a sunny place and trim back well in the autumn.

MINT (VARIOUS TYPES)

They are best planted in containers as the prolific varieties can take over your garden in no time. You can bury the pots but the roots are capable of breaking through and romping away. The three most common mints are spearmint, apple mint (Bowles is best for mint sauce) and peppermint.They are easy to grow and enjoy a sunny position.

SAGE

There are over 500 different types of sage and many are flowering garden plants. *Officinalis* is the best variety for cooking. The ancient Greeks and Romans used sage as a remedy for snake bites and as a general tonic. It will grow in most soils but prefers clay with good drainage and a sunny position. Cut it back well to encourage growth and harvest the sprigs before the flowers appear.

THYME

There are possibly 100 species of thyme, all developed from wild thyme. In ancient times, judges and the nobility carried thyme posies to protect them from diseases and the odour of the common people. Thyme is suitable for rock gardens and for growing between paving stones and on terraces. Brushing past and bruising the leaves releases their fragrance. Lemon thyme is my favourite; it's also popular with bees. Cutting back will encourage growth. In a cold winter, protect plants with a little straw.

ROSEMARY

It was said in ancient times that rosemary grew only in the gardens of the righteous. Thought to strengthen the memory, rosemary is a symbol of friendship. Buy a biggish plant, plant it in a sunny position and protect it from frost in the first winter. Rosemary is difficult to get going but once established will flourish for years. Large flowering spears look good in flower arrangements and super on a summer cheeseboard.

BAY LEAVES

From the sweet bay tree, often grown as a decorative shrub, the fresh leaves are great for cooking. A potted bay tree or cut sprigs can decorate the house at Christmas. Plant a small bay tree in a tub in good soil and place it in a sunny spot. Protect it in frosty weather. If you're lucky enough to have an established bay tree, it responds to a good pruning in the spring.

PARSLEY

It is a biennial and not easy to grow (for me, anyway). It is said that only a wicked woman or a woman who is master of the household can grow it successfully! There are two main types – curly and flat-leafed. Though flat-leafed parsley is more fashionable now, I prefer curly. Parsley likes some shade and a soil rich in humus. Keep it well watered in dry weather and keep harvesting the leaves and cutting back the stalks, otherwise the plants will flower and go to seed.

BASIL

An annual herb, basil cannot withstand frost but is easily grown from seed. The pleasure of growing your own is second to none. Plant the seeds in early spring (indoors or in the green-house) and prick out into individual pots in potting compost. You'll probably find that they all take and you'll be able to give some plants away. Keep in pots, either in the greenhouse or on a sunny windowsill. The leaves can burn in direct sun. Be sure to keep picking the leaves and nip out the top shoots to encourage bushy growth and prevent the plant from flowering.

TARRAGON

French tarragon is the only plant worth growing (Russian tarragon doesn't have the flavour or culinary uses). Tarragon is not an annual but is delicate and best treated as such. It likes well-drained soil that is not heavy and definitely no frost. It can be grown indoors in a pot in good light soil, but avoid over-watering. You don't need to water it more than once or twice a week.

TO PRESERVE HERBS

When cultivating herbs, it is worth remembering that the easiest ones to dry yourself are thyme (all types), bay leaves, rosemary and sage. Flavouring vinegar is another popular way of preserving your herb harvest. Basil loses its flavour easily and is the most difficult to preserve – making it into pesto (an Italian paste of basil with pine nuts, garlic, Parmesan cheese and olive oil) and then freezing the paste is successful and safe; or whizzing it (in a liquidizer) with olive oil and then freezing it is a good way of preserving the intense flavour.

TO DRY HERBS

Cut the stems as long as you can and tie into loose bunches with garden string, making a loop with the ends of the string. Hang upside down in a warm dark place – an airing cupboard is perfect. Dry until the leaves are brittle enough to crumble, take down carefully and remove the leaves. Store in airtight jars, labelled and dated, in a cool dark place. A year is long enough to keep them.

Allotments

ALLOTMENTS are available all over the country. Contact your local council to find out what they can offer and whether there is a waiting list.

Some councils have dedicated allotment officers who will be able to tell you all about annual fees, rules (for example, whether you can keep chickens or rabbits or even bees) and leasing arrangements. Costs are very reasonable, for example from £10 a year with a small charge for water. Leases are usually for a year. A standard allotment is usually 5 rods, with a rod also known as a perch or pole. This is an ancient measuring system in which 1 rod is equal to about 5 metres (5½ yards). Smaller lots can be obtained, or you may be able to share one and split the labour and cost.

TO TAKE ON AN ALLOTMENT

It is worth visiting the allotments on a Sunday afternoon when everyone will be toiling away and it is a good opportunity to find out all sorts of important information. Take advice from your fellow allotment holders, especially if you are new to vegetable gardening, they will have plenty of useful hints and tips. Be sure to ask as many questions as you need of the other tenants before taking on the allotment:

- What soil type is it? You can get a soil-testing kit from a garden centre.
- Is the ground ever waterlogged?
- Are some plots better than others?
- Is there any problem with vandalism?
- What are the rules about sheds?

● Is there good access to water?

● Do you pay extra for water, and do hose pipe bans apply?

● Does anyone have a rotivator (or even a tractor, if you know a friendly farmer) you can borrow to dig up your plot for sowing?

● Are there reduced rates for pensioners?

● Are you allowed to plant fruit trees?

● Is there an allotment society and do you pay towards it?

● Do they try to encourage mostly organic gardening?

● Do they hold an annual show?

● Are you allowed to sell produce, for example at a communal village stall?

Note: if you're going to take your young children, make sure there is a safe place to play or give them their own plot to dig.

WHAT TO GROW?

Most allotment holders grow vegetables and fruit on their plots, leaving the flowers to their gardens at home, but if you have a large plot, it can look beautiful at certain times of year with colourful blooms such as sunflowers or marigolds, or even a wild flower patch. Some flowers grow well with vegetables so check this out. Once you get your plot, you may find that it hasn't been touched for years and is a tangle of weeds, in which case clear it bit by bit. The best time to start doing this is autumn or early winter.

EDIBLE LEAVES AND FLOWERS

Young, bright green dandelion leaves are super in spring salads. You can also eat young nasturtium leaves (they taste a little like watercress) and the flowers, which have a milder flavour. You can use pansies, primroses, violets and marigolds as pretty decorations on puddings or in salads (they can also be eaten in salads).

THE FLOWER GARDEN

TO DEAD HEAD FLOWERS

During the summer, when your flowers are in full bloom, it's a good idea to dead head. If you have the patience and time to cut off flowers that are past their best, you'll see your plants continue to bloom. All plants want to do is reproduce themselves; by cutting off the flower heads you will be forcing them to send out more flowers and try again to produce seeds. Do this at least every other day and not only will you find it rewarding but you'll also discover that there's nothing more calming than wandering around your garden in the evening with a pair of secateurs. Cut off rose heads as though you are pruning, and perennials down to the ground; just take the heads off annuals.

ANNUALS

These are flowers that grow from seed and flower all in one year before they die. Most bedding plants are annuals and will flower until the first frosts.

BIANNUALS

These are planted one year to flower the next. They will usually continue to flower for a few years afterwards, but will be rather weak and poorly. Wallflowers are a good example of a biannual.

PERENNIALS

These flower every year. Plant these in a herbaceous border and every 4–5 years they will have grown to the extent that they can be divided (in the autumn). They are super to pass on to friends. Don't grow them from seed (best left to professional gardeners), but insead buy as plants or ask your gardening friends for a root.

SWEET-SMELLING FLOWERS

These are a special treat to grow and are often fragrant in the early evening, which makes sitting outside with a drink a great pleasure for the senses. The following are a selection of scented plants.

● **Annuals** Night-scented stocks, tobacco plants (Nicotiana) and sweet peas. Buy scented sweet peas (usually the old-fashioned varieties) as seeds and grow them on a tripod of bamboo canes.

● **Biannuals** Brompton stocks and some scented pinks; don't forget lily of the valley that flowers in early spring and can be cut and brought into the house.

● **Climbing plants** Honeysuckle – be sure to buy a sweet-smelling plant as some are not highly perfumed. Jasmine Officinale is an amazingly fragrant plant.

CLIMBING PLANTS

They look good growing up an old dead tree, small or large and make a good display on a trellis fence.

● *Montana clematis* grows quickly and blooms in the spring; other species of clematis, though they have huge exotic flowers, can be more difficult to grow.

● Climbing and rambling roses also look wonderful – go for fragrant types, such as Albertine, a pale coppery pink; Golden Showers in yellow; or Zephrine Drouhin, which is red, old-fashioned and highly fragrant. Buy from a specialist rose grower for a huge choice and good advice. It is often said that it is a good idea to buy roses from a supplier north of where you live as this gives them a good chance of growing well in your (more southerly) area.

RUSSIAN VINE

Consider this climber if you want to cover or disguise a fence or shed; however, it is so fast growing it could spread all over your garden and take over. It is a good quick fix to cover something ugly.

WILD FLOWERS

It is a good idea to leave a corner of your garden for wild flowers. You can buy packets of wild flower seeds – I have always found them difficult to germinate, which is strange really. You can sometimes buy plants (such as cowslips) in garden centres but another idea is simply to let wild flowers 'arrive', or if any other unorthodox plant seeds itself elsewhere in the garden transplant it to your wild area. Grasses are also interesting. Do remember not to add any fertilizers to your wild garden area.

BULBS

TO PLANT SMALL BULBS

If you stand at your kitchen sink and look out of the window, nothing can be more uplifting in early spring than the sight of snowdrops (they will flower first) and other small bulbs. As you will probably not be spending much time outside in the garden in early spring (not sitting around), try and plant spring bulbs where you will see them from the house.

TO DEAD HEAD SPRING BULBS

As soon as the flowers fade, remove them with secateurs. This ensures that the bulbs put their energy into next years flowers. Leave the leaves as they are – they will gradually turn yellow and can be cut back after 6 weeks. Don't tie the leaves into neat bundles.

TO TRANSPLANT HOUSE-POTTED HYACINTHS

Blue hyacinths have by far the strongest scent and often seem to be stronger plants. After they have flowered indoors, put them outside to die down naturally and then plant the bulbs in the garden where they will flower next year, and for many years afterwards. This works for bulbs you planted yourself and for bought flowering bulbs. You can build up quite a collection by planting them out; remember, you can also cut the hyacinths when in flower and bring them into the house. Crocuses and other small bulbs that have flowered in the house can be treated in the same way.

WILD FOOD

If you are seriously interested in wild foods, it is worth seeking out a book or two on the topic. Some modern classics include *Food for Free* by Richard Mabey (Fontana); *Wild Food* by Roger Phillips (Pan); and *Poisonous Plants and Fungi* by Marion R. Cooper and Anthony W. Johnson (Ministry of Agriculture Fisheries and Food). This last one indicates all sorts of upsets that can result from poor pickings (as well as potential problems for animals and livestock) but most importantly it tells and shows you the poisonous species to avoid. Ask a good secondhand bookshop to look out for out-of-print books on the subect or try one of the book search dealers on the internet.

BLACKBERRIES

There is no doubt that wild blackberries have far more flavour than cultivated varieties.

Unbelievably, there are at least 400 different micro-species of blackberry growing in Britain, all differing slightly in flavour, sweetness and ripening times.
● Pick from late August until the end of October. There is an old wives tale that the devil spits on blackberries after the end of September. Picking is earlier in hot summers. Try to avoid picking from brambles near busy roads.

TO FREEZE BLACKBERRIES

They freeze fantastically well, in lidded plastic containers. Even when frozen together you can remove as many as you need. They are best cooked with cooking apples (Bramley apples are best), half and half in pies and crumbles.

BLACKBERRY JAM AND JELLY

There is very little pectin (a natural setting agent present in some fruits) in blackberries so they are usually combined, half and half, with cooking apples for flavour and added tartness, as well as for a good set.

TO MAKE BLACKBERRY VINEGAR

This is an old recipe (so no metric measures!) that works wonderfully well. Put 1 lb blackberries (very ripe fruit works well) and 1 pint white wine vinegar in a bowl or large bottle. Cover well and leave to steep for about two weeks. Be sure to give the fruit a good shake or stir occasionally. Strain, put into a saucepan and add 1 lb sugar and 8 oz runny honey. Bring to the boil slowly, stirring until all the sugar and honey have dissolved. Cool and bottle the vinegar. Plastic tonic-type bottles are good. Screw the tops on well and store in a dark place. Great in gravies (especially with game) and casseroles; the sweet vinegar can be shaken over blackberries, strawberries or ice cream.

BILBERRIES

Mostly found in Scotland and Wales and in the north and west of England, these come from a low-growing shrub thriving on open moorland. They are small, luscious and juicy, not unlike blueberries; they can be used in the same way. The only drawback is that bilberries are back-breakingly difficult to pick and they stain your fingers.

WILD RASPBERRIES

You can find these in Britain, usually in June, pick with pleasure and use as cultivated ones.

BLACKCURRANTS, RED-CURRANTS AND GOOSEBERRIES

These can all be found growing wild in Britain, often as garden escapees. If you come across them, take advantage of the opportunity to pick as there is nothing more rewarding than food for free.

WILD STRAWBERRIES

Known in France as *fraise du bois*, you will need to search carefully during July and August to find these little ground-hugging plants bearing tiny strawberries. When you track them down you will discover that their flavour is intense and fragrant. Best eaten when you find them – if they are warmed by the sun, even better. If you have the patience to pick them, take some home; they are delicious with a little champagne poured over them.

ELDERFLOWERS

The scent of elderflowers is one of spring's most thrilling aromas. For generations they have been used in many ways and have once again become very fashionable. Gather elderflowers when they are in full bloom, cutting the heads with secateurs or scissors just behind the bloom. When you get them home, shake each bloom really well to remove any insects.

ELDERFLOWERS WITH GOOSEBERRIES

A marriage made in heaven. When cooking gooseberries for crumbles, pies, fools or jam, try adding a couple of elderflower heads for every 450 g (1 lb) fruit.

Add them with the water used to cook the fruit. Remove the heads afterwards and proceed as normal; you will be rewarded with a wonderful Muscat flavour.

ELDERFLOWER CHAMPAGNE

A refreshing, light and fizzy drink, reminiscent of champagne.

3 heads of elderflower, in full bloom
1 lemon
500 g (1 lb) sugar
2 tablespoons white vinegar
4-8 litres (8 pints) cold water

Squeeze the juice from the lemon and cut the rind into four. Put this with the other ingredients in a large china or plastic bowl or bucket (not metallic). Cover with a clean cloth and leave for 24 hours, then strain and pour into bottles with screw tops (tonic water bottles are good). Keep for at least 2 weeks and drink chilled. The champagne can be kept until September, but no longer.

ELDERBERRIES

Gather when the fruiting heads have turned black and juicy. You will be competing with the birds, usually during July and August. Use a fork to scrape the berries from the stalks and wash well. They can be used half and half with blackberries to make pies, jams and jellies. They are also excellent for making wine.

SLOES

The fruit of the blackthorn and a relation of cultivated plums, these are best used for sloe gin. Found in hedgerows, the tiny blue-black fruit ripens in September or October. Take care when picking as the bushes or trees have very sharp thorns. Don't be tempted to eat them – they are the most sour fruit you can imagine. Just remove all the leaves and twiggy bits, put in a polythene bag and freeze for 24 hours.

TO MAKE SLOE GIN/VODKA

For every pound (old recipe, so no metric) of sloes, take 1 lb sugar and 1 pint gin or vodka. I buy a cheap brand in a bottle with a wide neck so that the ingredients fit in easily. Place the bottle on a sunny window sill and give it a good shake two or three times a day. It should be ready by Christmas. Purists will tell you to keep it for another year, but there's no reason to do so.

DAMSONS

These wild plums or Bullace are not common. If you find a tree in a hedgerow, it is worth gathering any fruit you can. Not as large as cultivated plums, damsons are blue-black and just about sweet enough to eat raw. They are great for jam (see page 44). They ripen in late September and October.

NETTLES

Gather young nettles in the spring to make a lovely soup. They are reminiscent of sorrel in flavour. Don't forget to wear gloves when you pick them.

WALNUTS

If you are fortunate enough to have a walnut tree in your garden, or know of a wild one, you will find that the nuts ripen in late October or November. They can also be picked earlier in July, when they are known as green or wet walnuts. This is when they can be pickled, before their shells harden. It is a difficult process but I include a recipe as some people are addicted to them. NB When gathering wet walnuts your hands will become black and stained.

TO MAKE PICKLED WALNUTS

This old recipe for pickled walnuts predates metrication and the quantities are approximate. Start with about 2 lb nuts: they should be soft enough to pass a knitting needle or skewer through. Prick each one all over with a fork and soak in a brine made with 1 pint water and 4 tablespoons of salt. There should be enough brine to cover them comfortably. Leave for a week, until the nuts are black. Drain and rinse the nuts and let them dry for 2–3 days, laid out on a plastic tray and covered with a cloth. Pack the nuts into clean jars. Cover with hot pickling vinegar, home-made or bought. Cover and label the jars and leave to stand for at least a month before eating.

HAZELNUTS

These begin to ripen around September, about the same time as the leaves begin to turn yellow on the bushes. Try and get them before the squirrels. Keep them in a warm dry place in their shells.

MARSH SAMPHIRE

Found on salt marshes around British coasts, this has become fashionable in recent years, particularly served with fish in more expensive restaurants. Picked in June and July the young shoots can be eaten raw in salads: the nearest flavour comparison is a slightly salty asparagus. The older plants, picked in August or September, can be lightly boiled and eaten with melted butter in the same way as asparagus.

WATERCRESS

If you have the opportunity to pick wild watercress, do so; the pleasure of eating it fresh and tangy is wonderful. It makes fantastic soup too. But care must be taken to pick from clean, fast-flowing streams that do not flow through pasture land with grazing sheep or cattle.

WILD FENNEL

Often found growing on waste ground in damp, sunny places near the sea, you will recognise fennel by the feathery leaves on 1.5-metre (5 foot) high plants. Crush a little between your fingers to release the smell of aniseed. Only the leaves are to be used; the plump white fennel bulbs in the greengrocers are from a different, cultivated plant (known as Florence fennel). Gather the fronds and use fresh, especially with fish. Fennel can be dried – hang bunches in an airing cupboard. The seeds, gathered in October, can be chewed and are popular after Indian meals, when they can help to prevent wind.

WILD FUNGI

Picking wild mushrooms is a wonderful and rewarding pastime – be careful you may become addicted to mushroom hunting!

You must know what you are doing. There are good reference books (*Mushrooms* by Roger Phillips is excellent) and a great website for all mushroom info. (www.mycologue.co.uk), but it is preferable to have someone with you who knows what's what. It's a good idea to go on a mushroom hunt with a local expert first (many are available around the country) as this will help with basic identification and give you an idea of how to start out. They will also advise on organisations or individuals who provide a checking service – if you pick something you're not sure of, you may be able to get it checked for future reference.

Mushrooms are the most fascinating of wild foods. There are at least 3,000 different types of fungi in Britain, and there are no exact rules about where they grow. The weather is important and a damp warm autumn is perfect. Just because a particular fungi grew in one place last year it doesn't mean it will be there this year. Some mushrooms appear early in the year (June), but most are harvested from late August until the first frosts.

Early morning is the best time for picking, and you'll be competing with all sorts of creatures and insects who enjoy eating mushrooms.

The following are some good examples of mushroom species to look out for.

CHANTERELLE
These are very valuable mushrooms and to find them is a real thrill. They are the most beautiful egg-yolk yellow and funnel shaped, common in woodlands, especially among dry beech leaves and on mossy banks.

FIELD OR WOOD BLEWITS
Field blewits are not uncommon in grassy open pastures and sometimes on cliff tops near the sea. They have a slightly 'jellyish' feel to them and a blue-violet stem. Wood blewits are similar, though their stems are not as brightly coloured and they are found in deciduous woodlands.

PARASOL MUSHROOM
They actually look like little parasols and cannot be mistaken for anything else. Tall – about 18 cm (7 in) and speckled brown like an egg, they are often found in wood margins, grassy clearings and at the edges of fields.

FIELD MUSHROOMS
These are the mushrooms that are related to those we buy in the shops, though there are many different types and sizes, and not all of them are edible. Mostly found in open fields and meadows, field mushrooms have more flavour than the shop-bought varieties.

CEP, PORCINI OR PENNY BUN

These are exotic, expensive and wonderful to eat. A good chef would almost kill to find some growing wild! They are different from other fungi in that the underneath of the cap looks more like a sponge, unlike the gills under other mushrooms. There are many varieties in this family. Penny bun is so named because it looks like an uncrossed hot-cross bun – sort of brown and shiny. They are found mostly in woods (especially beech) in dappled, sunny clearings, sometimes next to paths and areas where horses are ridden, and occasionally on the edges of golf courses. They are very popular with insects, so check them well before cooking.

GIANT PUFFBALL

If you find a giant puffball it is impossible to mistake it for anything else. These can grow to be bigger than a football! White, smooth and leathery looking, the giant puffball eventually turns yellow-brown and becomes dry. Gather at the white stage. It is difficult to say exactly where they like to grow; they seem to appear on quiet road verges, under hedges and at field edges. When you see your first puffball it is a magical moment. There is no need to peel a puffball – just give it a good brush and cut it into thick slices.

TO DRY MUSHROOMS

Mushrooms can be dried very successfully. One way is to thread them on thick cotton (use a large needle), like a string of beads, and hang them up in a dry, airy place.

TO COOK WILD MUSHROOMS

They are great in omelettes or fried in butter with a touch of garlic, and a squeeze of lemon.

PICKING TIPS

- Do be 100 per cent sure that you are picking an edible specimen. Accurate identification is vital.
- Take a basket or trug to gather mushrooms; don't use plastic bags, which allow the fungi to get damp and sweaty.
- Avoid picking on very wet days. Fungi are very porous and will soak up water quickly, this will spoil the taste and texture.
- To pick, either twist the mushroom stalk gently until it breaks, or invest in a specialist mushroom knife. A small to medium, sharp and fairly strong kitchen knife will work.
- To make sure they continue to grow, treat the fungi with care – don't tug them up from the ground or twist them violently, and try not to disturb the mycelium (the network from which they grow) too much. Leave some fungi to cast their spores.
- Go through all the mushrooms carefully before cooking and try not to wash them; a large, soft make-up brush is excellent for brushing away any earth or little insects.

Serve with crusty bread to mop up the juices. Puffballs are good sliced and fried with bacon for breakfast; parasols too. They can both be coated with egg and breadcrumbs and fried until crisp; and don't forget mushroom soup. Look out for an Antonio Carluccio mushroom cookery book – he is an expert and his books offer numerous good picking tips and recipes.

TO DEEP FRY MUSHROOMS

Make a fairly thick but light batter with lager beer, plain flour, salt and freshly ground black pepper. Use mushrooms whole or cut into large chunks. Dip them into the batter, shake to remove the excess and deep fry in hot sunflower oil. They will rise to the surface when they are done. Drain well on kitchen paper and enjoy.

SAFE FUNGI

As a final note to finish this section, I feel that I must again point out how important it is to know what mushrooms you are picking. It is sometimes said that for every edible wild fungi, there is a poisonous type that looks very similar – you just need to know the little differences. If in doubt, don't touch or pick it.

OUTDOOR EATING

SUMMER BARBECUES

They're easy and good fun, and there's no better feeling than eating food that you've cooked for yourself outdoors. There is definitely an art to getting the coals to the right temperature so that the food is cooked through and not burnt on the outside and raw in the middle. Unfortunately we have all experienced this at sometime or other!

CHOICE OF BARBECUE

There are two basic types of barbecue, either charcoal or gas, both working on the same principal. Gas is the quickest to heat up but more expensive while charcoal (my choice) is more primitive, exciting and 'hands on'.

There are many different sizes of barbecue and you need to take this into consideration when buying. If you are someone who will only barbecue once or twice a year, something small and simple may be the best choice. If you will be taking it to the beach, look for one that is transportable. If you buy a large barbecue make sure that you have room in a garage or shed to store it, or that it has a suitable weatherproof cover.

You can build your own barbecue so that it is a permanent fixture in the garden, but make sure you site it in a sheltered place away from overhanging plants and wooden fences. Build it with a few bricks in two stacks and balance a grill between them - easy!

TO SITE YOUR BARBECUE

It is most important to position the barbecue on a flat, wobble-free surface. It is handy to have room for a small table nearby to lay out cooking implements, oven gloves and all the other bits and pieces you may need.

THE SECRET OF GOOD BARBECUING

....is a good fire and controlling the heat. You can use specialist eco-friendly wood chips (see below), or you can use lump wood charcoal, which can be bought impregnated with a lighting agent, or charcoal briquettes, which take longer to light but tend to burn longer. To make sure that you are buying charcoal from sustainable forests look out for the FSC (Forest Stewardship Council) logo.

ECO-FRIENDLY AND FLAVOUR-IMPARTING SMOKE

You can burn a variety of materials to flavour the food. Dry twigs from fruit trees and fresh woody herbs (such as rosemary, thyme and bay leaves) work well. You can use specialist wood chips, including hickory, mesquite, oak, apple, and chips made from old whisky barrels. They should all be soaked in water or a mixture of water and beer for 30 minutes before putting on the hot charcoal. The soaking causes the wood to smoulder rather than burst into flames and burn too quickly. For a gas barbecue they should be rolled in a sheet of foil (into a sausage shape), which should be pricked with a skewer to allow the smoke to escape.

TO LIGHT YOUR BARBECUE

There are various types of fire lighters especially designed for barbecues (as they don't give off fumes). Do not use domestic fire lighters as they contain paraffin which will taint your food. There are also barbecue lighter fluids, which are odourless, but care must be taken with these. Electric starters are available but you must have a power point nearby or a long extension lead.

GETTING READY TO COOK

Allow at least 45 minutes from lighting for a charcoal barbecue to reach cooking temperature. A gas barbecue will be ready in 10 minutes. Before starting, make sure that all your food will be ready to cook when the barbecue is hot. Pile the charcoal into a pyramid and tuck the fire lighter in below. Light and leave until the coals are glowing red – about 5–10 minutes.

Rake the coals into an even layer and leave until the flames have disappeared and the coals are glowing with a dusty-white ash on them. The best temperature for most cooking is when there is a fairly thick white ash on the coals. As a guide, you should be able to hold your hand about 15 cm (6 in) above the fire for about 5 seconds.

ADJUSTING THE COOKING TEMPERATURE

You can knock some of the ash off the coals and push them closer together for more heat. To cool down the barbecue, spread out the coals. You can also lower or raise the cooking rack to vary the temperature and speed of cooking. If you're cooking for more than an hour, you will need to add more coals; rake the hot coals together and add fresh charcoal to the outer edges.

SAFETY TIPS

- Don't barbecue in high winds.
- Never barbecue indoors.
- Once the barbecue is lit, don't leave it unattended.
- Keep children and animals away from the barbecue.
- NEVER light a barbecue with paraffin, petrol or white spirit; not only is this extremely dangerous, but it will also taint the food.

TO CLEAN A BARBECUE

Clean up after every cooking session, removing any bits of food. Follow the manufacturer's instructions, where necessary. Before you put the barbecue away, brush off as much stuck on food as you can with a wire brush – the type designed for cleaning an Aga is particularly good. Then use a strong solution of washing soda (renowned for removing grease) by adding 1 cup soda crystals to 600 ml (1 pint) hot water. Wear rubber gloves, scrub the racks and rinse them well.

COOKING HINTS

- When cooking on skewers, try not to push the pieces of food on too closely – allow space between them for even cooking.
- Remember to soak wooden skewers in cold water for at least 30 minutes before using them, otherwise they burn easily.
- Use a little oil to brush the cooking racks lightly – this helps to prevent the food from sticking to them.
- After marinating food, try to scrape off some of the marinade before cooking. It drips on to the coals and makes them flare up and this burns the food.
- Always have a spray bottle of water handy to put out flare-ups.
- If you are cooking in foil (garlic bread or fish, for example) always use the extra-thick foil.

COOKING TIMES

These times are only approximate. All pieces of meat, chicken and fish are a different thickness. The temperature and rack position will influence the cooking time. A good test is to cut into one of the larger pieces to check if is cooked all the way through. You can pop things into an oven if they are brown but not quite cooked; this does defeat the object but means that you have not got burnt food still undercooked in the middle and you still have the barbecue flavour. (Using the oven as back-up is a good idea if you are barbecuing for a crowd.

Fish: allow 10 minutes per 2.5-cm (1 in) flesh thickness, turning once. It is very easy to overcook fish and it will soon become dry and tasteless.

Prawns: (large and whole, raw in shell) 4–6 minutes, turning halfway through.

Boneless chicken thighs and breasts: 12–14 minutes, turning halfway through.

Chicken drumsticks, breasts and thighs on the bone: 20-25 minutes, turning regularly.

Beef steaks: 3-4 minutes each side for rare; 4-5 minutes each side for medium; 5-6 minutes each side for well done.

Beef burgers: 3-4 minutes each side for rare; 5-6 minutes each side for medium; 6-8 minutes each side for well done.

Lamb chops: 12–14 minutes, turning halfway through.

Lamb fillet: 9–10 minutes, turning halfway through.

Pork (boneless): 14–16 minutes, turning halfway through.

Pork chops: 16–20 minutes, turning halfway through.

Pork fillet: (whole) 25 minutes, turning regularly.

Sausages: 8–10 minutes, turning regularly.

TO MAKE A BASIC MARINADE

This is useful for swordfish, fresh tuna, chicken, lamb, vegetables and Haloumi cheese (a Cypriot cheese that forms a golden skin when grilled). Mix 2 crushed garlic cloves, with the grated zest and juice of 1 lemon, 1 tablespoon of dried oregano or 2 tablespoons of fresh lemon thyme, 2 teaspoons of runny honey, 4 tablespoons of olive oil and salt and freshly ground black pepper.

Marinate the meat or chicken for up to 24 hours. fish or vegetables for 2 hours. Use a shallow non-metallic dish so that the food can be laid out in a single layer, cover it well and place in the fridge.

TO MAKE A BASIC SALSA

Mix together 2 peeled and finely chopped tomatoes, 1 seeded and finely chopped fresh green chilli, 1 finely chopped spring onion, the juice of 1 lime and chopped fresh coriander leaves. Add a little salt and taste to check the seasoning (don't add pepper because of the chilli) and leave to stand for 30 minutes for the flavours to meld together. You can add a peeled, stoned and chopped ripe avocado to this salsa.

FOR PUDDING

Top and tail a fresh pineapple and slice off the sides to remove the skin and prickly bits. Cut into rings, remove the core and lightly grind black pepper over each side. Pop on the grill at the end of cooking, for about 3 minutes on each side. Serve with vanilla ice cream and a splash of Kirsch.

NEED MORE BARBECUE IDEAS?

There are lots of dishes to cook on the barbecue; for example, try tandoori chicken on page 48. For lots of recipe ideas, treat yourself to a specialist barbecue book or borrow one from the library. Ainsley Harriott and Jamie Oliver have great advice and recipes for cooking outside.

PICNICS

There is no better way to celebrate a summer's day than by having a picnic, either in your garden or on a jaunt in the country or to the seaside. You can enjoy really good picnic food without too much fuss, especially as we are not always sure how the weather will turn out. You don't want to prepare all sorts of exotic food for something that may not happen. Simplicity, ease of transport, and non-leak containers are the keys to success.

WHAT TO TAKE?

Take a large blanket or similar for everyone to sit on and cushions if you like – or even folding chairs.

Use chiller boxes to carry the food and keep it fresh. You can include some cutlery but it is often not necessary so long as you make sure you have at least one sharp knife should you want to cut bread, for example. Take plastic glasses; and remember the bottle opener, if you are having wine.

Have a supply of paper napkins and moist wipes to clean hands and fingers. Pack insect repellent, and sting-relief spray is also a good idea. Lastly, do not leave any rubbish or mess behind – pack a rubbish sack so that you can take it home with you or put it into the appropriate bins.

BAGUETTE OR ROLL IDEAS

Slit a small crusty brown or white baguette or a crusty roll horizontally and fill generously. Cut in half and wrap well in greaseproof paper and foil. Allow one per person.

- Fill with cream cheese, freshly torn basil leaves, season with salt and freshly ground black pepper.
- Fill with grated cheddar cheese mixed with mayonnaise and grated carrot – unusual but good.
- Slices of ripe brie and halved seedless black grapes are also excellent in a baguette.

SANDWICHES AND OTHER PICNIC FOOD

See page 62 of Food and Entertaining for sandwich ideas. As a rule, don't use meat fillings – there is nothing worse than warm ham, salami or beef! Tomatoes make sandwiches soggy too.

Hard-boiled eggs: leave them in their shells and take some Maldon salt or celery salt to dip them in.

Cucumber sticks: take toasted sesame seeds as a dip.

Cheese and celery: cube some really good Cheddar and serve wih washed and cut-up celery sticks.

Cherry tomatoes: Gardeners Delight are best and, again, take along some Maldon salt to sprinkle on them.

Sausages: cold, cooked pork sausages are really good outdoor food. Wrap them individually, and take some mustard or tomato ketchup with you for dipping purposes.

TAKE A CAKE

A good moist light fruit cake (see Coombe cake, page 39) always goes down well or try the Banana and Chocolate Chip Cake from the Food and Entertaining chapter (page 66). Cut the cake into slices and wrap individually in cling film.

ICED TEA

Make tea in the usual way but with half as much water as normal. When it's cool, pour into a vacuum flask with ice cubes and a few sprigs of mint (add a little sugar if you like). The ice will melt on the journey.

CHILLING THE WINE

If you like your wine chilled and you're by a river or at the seaside, you can cool it in the water. Tie string around the neck of the bottle and let it dangle in the running water. Don't forget alcohol-free drinks for the driver. Home-made lemonade is refreshing and goes down well with children and adults.

HOW TO MAKE LEMONADE

Pour 600 ml (1 pint) water into a saucepan and add 2 tablespoons granulated sugar. Bring to the boil and check that all the sugar has dissolved – the syrup should be completely clear. Meanwhile, cut 2 lemons in half, squeeze out all the juice and place in a bowl with the skins. Cool the sugar syrup for 5 minutes and then pour it over the lemons. Cover, leave until cold and chill thoroughly. Strain to serve. This is very refreshing and cooling, and the less sugar you add the better. Experiment with the quantities to find the proportions you prefer.

ORANGE AND CHOCOLATE CHIP COOKIES

125 g (4 oz) butter or margarine
100 g (3 oz) sugar
125 g (4 oz) self-raising flour
50 g (2 oz) oats
½ teaspoon bicarbinate of soda
    grated rind of 1 orange
50 g (2 oz) chocolate chips

1. Either put everything into the food processor and whiz (on pulse) until the mixture just comes together OR
cream the fat and sugar and mix in all the other ingredients. In both cases you will need to bring the dough together with your hands.

2. Divide the biscuit dough into 16 and roll each piece into a ball. Place these on a greased baking sheet and press down lightly on each ball with the back (tines) of a fork. The biscuits will spread out as they cook.
3. Bake for 20/25 minutes at Gas 5/190 C/375°F until golden. Leave for a few moments on the tray and then remove to a cooling rack.
Note: the biscuits will crisp up as they cool and keep well in a tin, if you can esist eating them all at once!

VITAL CONTACTS

Listed on these pages are some useful contacts (in no particular order) to help you cope with life.

Where to find cheap flights. A non-affiliated search engine that will direct you to the company offering the cheapest tickets.
www.traveljungle.co.uk

Where to checkout the cheapest car insurance.
www.insure121.com

Where to discover the value of a vehicle.
www.theaa.com

To hire a car anywhere in the world.
www.carrentals.co.uk
Telephone: 0845 225 0845

Directions to any UK street:
www.multimap.com

To discover specialist cycle routes in your area.
www.sustrans.org.uk

To get rid of junk calls:
www.tpsonline.org.uk

A website designed to save money (not guaranteed!).
www.moneysavingexpert.com

To safely recycle mobile phones.
The Body Shop has freepost bags; Oxfam and Scope have unwanted phones schemes

To recycle old spectacles for those in developing countries.
Dolland & Aitchinson, opticians

A company that provides cleaning staff UK wide.
www.merrymaids.co.uk

A web site for designer and celebrity clothes at high street prices:
www.asos.com

How to avoid using expensive 0870 numbers.
www.saynotoo870.com

To buy Fairtrade tea, coffee and drinking chocolate. Also, for a free magazine, *The Teapot Times.*
Telephone: 0800 169 3552
www.clipperteasshop.com

If you are thinking of keeping chickens, find information on:
Telephone: 0845 450 2056
www.omlet.co.uk

To order a weekly or fortnightly vegetable box:
Delivered to your door with seasonal organic fruit and produce. Also a list of local and nationwide suppliers:
www.alotoforganics.co.uk

To order fresh fish from Cornwall.
A local, family-run business since 1947, based in St Ives, will deliver fresh fish, suitably packed, to your door.
www.mstevensandson.co.uk

To complain about unsatisfactory goods.
Contact the supplier first, in writing, then write to:
Office of Fair Trading,
Fleetbank House,
2-6 Salisbury Square,

London EC4Y 8JX
Telephone 0207 211 8000

Advertising standards authorities:
www.asa.org.uk

Basic health questions answered:
www.nhsdirect.nhs.uk

More info about the NHS:
www.drfoster.co.uk

To get cheaper prescriptions (if you pay).
Either a pre-payment or a season certificate is available, if you need more than five prescriptions in four months or more than 14 prescriptions in one year
Telephone 0845 850 0030 to buy over the phone with credit or debit card OR ask at the Post Office

The National Childbirth Trust (NCT): www.nctpregnancyandbabycare.com

For a congratulatory message from The Queen.
These include 60th, 65th, 70th wedding anniversaries and every anniversary following. For birthdays 100th and 105th and all following!
    Application forms from: The Anniversaries Office, Buckingham Palace, London SW1A 1AA

– no sooner than three weeks before the celebration date.

Information and support for people with cancer
This service is for sufferers, family and friends. Cancer specialist nurses will answer the phone, and there is good information on the web site.
Freephone: 0808 800 1234 (Mon-Fri: 9 a.m to 8 p.m)
www.cancerbacup.org.uk

Index of births, marriages and deaths:
www.1837online.com

To trace family ancestry.
www.nationalarchives.gov.uk

To trace family history.
www.familyrecords.gov.uk/frc

To request a copy of a will.
Write to: York Probate, Sub-Registry, First Floor, Clifford Street, York YO1 9RG
    State the full name of the deceased, date of birth, date of death, and last known address. Enclose a cheque for £5, made payable to:
H M Paymaster General.

For information about living wills and alternative funerals, contact:
Natural Death Centre,
6 Blackstock Mews,
Blackstock Road,
London N4 2BT
Telephone: 0871 288 2098.

To complain about gas and electricity suppliers,
or for independent advice:
Energywatch Consumer Helpline: 0845906 07 08

To compare gas and electricity prices
www.dailyquote.co.uk .

To buy books on the internet:
www.bookkoob.co.uk

Talking books (for the blind and partially sighted)
www.talkingbooks.co.uk

To find a home for unwanted items:
www.freecycle.org
This is a great way to find a good home for something you don't want You can request stuff too, and it's completely free.

Help and support for the elderly or their carers
www.ageconcern.org.uk
www.helptheaged.org.uk

Good value car parking at all British airports (non-affiliated)
www.parking4less.co.uk

The Law Society
www.lawsociety.org.uk

Post office users national council
www.dti.gov.uk/postal

171

INDEX